15.

Famous Flaws

Famous Flaws

Alice Loomer, Ph.D.

Macmillan Publishing Co., Inc.
NEW YORK

Collier Macmillan Publishers
LONDON

Macmillan Publishing Co., Inc.
866 Third Avenue, New York, N.Y. 10022
Collier Macmillan Canada, Ltd.

Library of Congress Cataloging in Publication Data

Loomer, Alice.
  Famous flaws.

  Includes index.
    1. Medicine—Cases, clinical reports, statistics.
2. Biography.   3. Physically handicapped—
Biography.   4. Deformities—Cases, clinical re-
ports, statistics.
I. Title.
R703.L66   616'.09   76-8411
ISBN 0-02-575101-8

First Printing 1976

Printed in the United States of America

To R. S.

*Who once long ago was a small
boy who wet the bed*

Contents

Acknowledgments

MY THANKS ARE DUE:

First, of course, to the remarkable libraries of New York, from the Research Branch of the Public Library to the John Jay College of Criminal Justice, but particularly to the magnificent historical collection of the New York Academy of Medicine and to Mrs. Weaver of their Malloch Rare Book Collection, who many times in our search was helpful well beyond the call of duty. To the historical societies and the many organizations for the disabled (including the American Leprosy Missions, which surprisingly gave us a James Bond story).

To Marian Mulroney, on whose shoulders fell much of the library research—an extraordinary researcher who combines persistence, judgment, and humor in just the right proportions. Without her, the project would have been a nightmare.

To my friends Carl Battaglia and Stephen Frommer, who studied the typescript and made valuable suggestions; to Robert Blair, who helped in the early stages of the research; and to Margretta Collins, who gave days of her lifelong expertise with the English language, making the revisions of typescript and correction of proofs a companionable task and far easier than it would otherwise have been. I recommend such friends and hasten to add that the flaws that remain in the book reflect only the recalcitrance of the author toward friend and editor alike.

Finally, to Celestyna Piaszczynski who, with the patience of any four of her favorite saints, kept the environmental chaos within bounds, my gratitude—and my love.

Introduction

You MAY NOT think so as you wind your way through Lord Byron's menagerie or George Washington's ordeals with his sea horse teeth, but this is a very serious-minded book. Tragedies have befallen the bodies of famous men and history has recorded their reactions in triumph and defeat: Roosevelt with his polio; Beethoven never hearing the Glorious Ninth except in his own head; Richard III made villainous by his twisted arm and back (*if* you believe Shakespeare; history buffs swear it's all a lie).

Be Richard as he may, major physical afflictions of the famous have often decided the course of history. But the fate of nations has also often hung on lesser bodily ailments: Wilson's indigestion at Versailles; Napoleon's drowsiness before the gates of Moscow, or his poor hemorrhoids that made him late for the Battle of Waterloo.

People suffering from serious disabilities have many in-

spirational examples to see them through whatever horror
fate has stuffed down their throats. But it's nice to have
noble company for the nittier mortifications of the body
also.

I have sat with hundreds of men, women, and even
children as they came to terms with some of the worst in-
sults the human body can take and survive: the motor-
cyclist's broken neck; the limbs severed under subway
trains; the strokes that leave dynamic men helpless. And,
strangely, after the first months or weeks of shock, it was
often not the global tragedy of a ruptured life that ground
the spirit but the trivia of physical incapacity: the inability
to turn a door knob or scratch one's own head when it
itched, or the expense of buying two pairs of shoes for one
pair of feet no longer the same size. And research unex-
pectedly revealed that people with smaller disabilities
often found them harder to adjust to than larger impairments. Some of the most painful emotional suffering I've
ever watched was caused by physical defects that needn't
have caused more than a mild chagrin. For nowhere is one
more tempted to idiocy than in appraising the significance
of flaws in that most precious of all possessions, our own
bodies. Psychotherapists can cite examples from their patients (and their own lives if they are honest enough)
where moles (or buck teeth or short penises) have been
transformed into mountains of misery. Women really believe that being overweight dooms one to go through life
unloved (an attitude that may make one go through life as
unloving and unlovable as the woman who kept her mouth
clamped grimly shut for fear a welcoming smile would
reveal her poor teeth). And I once knew a boy who killed
himself, an act motivated in part because he didn't like his
hair. God knows, there is enough pain in the world and in

our lives without adding to it by our own nonsense. I have seen how unnecessarily and how grievously people can be hurt when they lose perspective about the physical flaws that nature or accident has handed them.

So this is a tale not of tragedies but of the smaller tribulations of the flesh that plague us all, along with a good deal of gossip from high places and plenty of comfort for every adolescent who ever looked at a new crop of acne and wished he were dead; for every woman afraid of the moment of truth that reveals a flat chest; for every man grieving for a departed hairline or embarrassed by the men's room; for every child scorned by its campmates for being too small or too awkward, or for wetting the bed.

We've got unlikely-looking ladies who toppled thrones, and recipes for competing amorously against larger, handsomer, and terribly virile competition. We'll find out what lifestyles are available if you happen to be a boy with a lame foot (from utter reprobate to Supreme Court justice); how to be London's most loved woman (and a real sexpot) if you also happen to be London's ugliest; how to be a major league football player with or without toes; how to get your era's greatest actress to fall besottedly in love with you and support you for years even though you are squatty, completely hairless, pockmarked, have forty-eight pairs of drawers (with lace and other embellishments), and are a large, if not economy-sized, bastard.

By observing how an unromantic-looking man can be remembered as a famous lover; how a plain woman can inspire undying passion; how a homely child can grow into a beauty; how a weedy youth can become a strong leader; by noting, in fact, the realities of people and their lives, we can devise ways of living well with our own flaws. What proves to be lovable is often very different

from the stereotype, and what is strongly masculine can
be a far cry from the traditional he-man image.

Beauty and physical perfection are a gratification to the
ego and a joy to the eye. They do not, however, determine the quality of a life, an obvious fact often over-
looked. Even the Department of Health, Education, and
Welfare proclaimed grandly in a television commercial
that "The Future Belongs To The Physically Fit." In
which case, the future will be very different from the past.
That has sometimes belonged to the lame, the halt, and
the blind, and usually belonged to the itchy, the achy, and
the lumpy. We won't, apparently, be having any more
presidents like Roosevelt, Taft, Eisenhower, Johnson, or
Kennedy (were there *any* physically fit presidents?); no
more writers like Homer or Goethe; no more Darwins, or
Mozarts. But somehow I go on thinking that fame and life
will still be big enough to encompass a good many physical flaws without serious mishap.

So, enjoy another telling of woman's and man's infinite
variety from the Olympian heights of your own physical
perfection; if not, have a good time in the company of
your fellow sufferers. And beware of a passion for gingerbread or you too, like Thomas Carlyle, may come to grief.

Famous Flaws

From Mane
to Plain

$\mathcal{M}$ANY ANIMALS EXCITE US immediately by their beauty. Man is not one of them. Architecturally unsound, built to walk on all fours, with the impertinence to walk on two, he is by his genus alone considerably handicapped in appearance. Many living creatures merit our admiration—the grace of deer, the gold of fish or finch, the poetry in motion of every seagull, the song of any nightingale, the softness of a lamb. Few humans give such esthetic pleasure to eye or ear.

Perhaps because his species has so little, man has always worshipped physical beauty and grieved at badges of his own individual imperfections. Of all his obvious deficits, none makes him more of a laughing stock to more richly endowed organisms than his pitiful lack of a sleek pelt or gorgeous plumage. He, alas, must make do with a few little tufts of fur in odd places, and when his best effort, his crowning glory, the hair of his head, when even that departs from him and leaves him bald, he can be very sad indeed.

For the human race has a thing about hair. Over the centuries and geography of the world, hair has been on its mind. How much hair should a high-class citizen have? What color? Curly or straight? Braided? Teased? What is its spiritual meaning? These and many other solemn issues about hair still await their final answers.

Man draws his gods with luxuriant hair: Zeus and Thor; Jupiter and Neptune. And all the sun gods with their haloes of light transformed by man's imagination into golden, magnificent hair: the Babylonian and the Persian sun gods; and those of the Aztecs and the Mexicans; Golden Apollo of the Greeks; the Egyptian Ra; and the early Aryan sun gods in rich, thick (if occasionally frowsy) locks. And, of course, Jehovah (although there are questions about that as we shall see).

So hair is precious stuff and its loss not to be taken lightly. Even the cutting of hair has always been a risk, for the soul and brain lie directly under it and may be disturbed when hair is tampered with. The Mikados thought it wisest to have theirs cut when they were asleep. The soul, being safely out of the body on its dream adventures, would not be around to take offence. A chief of the Fiji clan took the precaution of eating a man for lunch to give him strength for the dangerous onslaught (with the primitive cutting tools, it was, if not dangerous, at least harrowing). With the Maoris, haircuts brought on thunder and lightning.

Freud, the spoilsport, said, nothing of the kind; they merely bring on castration anxiety. The Brahmins also think hair and sex go together and announce their sexual intent by the way they wear their hair: tonsured tuft for sexual restraint, a complete shave for celibacy, and, being inconsistent like everybody else about hair, symbolize a total detachment from sexual passion by unkempt hair. Celibate monks, in general, have tended to shave their heads. Many other people have shaved it off as a mark of grief or even torn it out in their despair, like the patriarchs of ancient Israel, or Sir Ralph the Rover in the cautionary Victorian verse about the fatal end of villains.

Hair has many uses: protection from sun and rain and cold, as well as cushioning the skull against the neighboring caveman. It can be shaken defiantly in the face of an enemy, and is an absolute prerequisite if you wish to kill lions bare-handed; witness Samson, Hercules, the Assyrian Gilgamesh, and the Phoenician Melpath. There is no evidence that it made them equally strong in the head.

Hair has often been deemed essential for power over men as well as lions. A ruler of the Franks, for example, automatically lost his power with a haircut. Forever. The hair might grow back. The power never. When throne-grabbing kidnappers of her young grandsons offered Queen Clotilda their lives or their hair, to live disgraced or die unshorn, she decreed the boys must die. Many American fathers a few years ago felt almost as strongly: better death than *long* hair.

But a lack of hair can also be a mark of leadership, as with the Egyptian Pharaohs. And if a man look for divine guidance in this matter, the gods have never been able to make up their minds either. There have often been divine commands not to get haircuts, and many holy men have shown their obedience, but other holy men have regarded it as a mortal sin. William, Archbishop of Rouen, in 1099 banned men with long hair from the churches and if they died still stubborn in the evil of their long hair, no prayers were to be said for their souls.

No question, hair is very significant (although significant of what, nobody knows). When the typical young man (one Western Caucasian in five will be bald by the age of thirty) discovers in his mirror that sizable numbers of his 100,000 hairs are leaving never to return, it is not a happy day. (Blonds have more not only fun but hair, and, shades of Rapunzel, a single head of hair can support the weight of two hundred people.) Of course, he has been losing and sprouting fifty to one hundred hairs a day all along, but this is different. (One lucky man in five will still have his hair in old age.)

Even kings and conquerors have been upset by their mirrors, and taken gratefully to laurel wreath and crown. Caesar's soldiers sang proudly of his bald head as a mark of his virility (or specifically, lechery), but Caesar himself liked the blank filled in by the leaves of fame.

Louis XIII, bald by the time he was twenty-three, was so chagrined he wore a wig even though they were in the Middle Ages thought to be a sign of the devil (what wasn't?). His courtiers naturally followed suit. Louis XIV, the Sun King, had had a beautiful head of fair hair and regarded early baldness as such a total affront to the royal dignity that he refused to be seen without his wigs. Even his valet was not allowed to gaze upon the humiliating vacancy but must hand the hairpieces through the royal bed curtains. Whatever his procession of mistresses saw, whether wig awry or cranial nudity, none of them ever seems to have leaked to the historians. Louis also admired wisdom and favored the powdered wig for its look of wise age, so everybody at court set out to look as old and wise as possible, and the powder flew.

But Charles II of England (the one who never said a foolish thing) preferred to conceal the wise grayness of his hair under youthful curly locks and, presto, wigs were the rage in England too. Six-year-olds wore them on Sundays and holidays, and servants packed suitable hairpieces for young masters off to aristocratic boarding schools.

Alas for the burgeoning wig industry, there came a scandalous time during the reign of George III (ontoward things were always happening during the reign of George III) when men began to appear right out in public without their wigs. The Barbers' Guild of London, outraged, staged a protest march and petitioned the king (on whom petitions habitually made little impact) beseeching that the wearing of wigs be enforced by law. George, in a fit of sanity, rejected their plea.

Wigs were also popular in the American colonies (the president of Harvard called them horrid bushes of fashion) although they rarely achieved the ornamental grandeur of the French and English nobility. They were also used for the practical purpose of covering whatever branding or earlopping one had encountered in the process of hog-stealing or non-church attending in early New England. Slaves in the South sometimes fashioned their own from cotton and goat hair.

Eventually different styles came to symbolize different callings, for "who, in this enlightened age, would put the least confidence in a physician who wears his own hair." The barristers of England hold to a similar point of view, appearing in court to this day in the most unappetizing of Jacobin wigs.

So with all kinds of ancestral preoccupations with hair buzzing around in his unconscious, it's not surprising that modern man gets shook up when he realizes that, in

numbering his hair, the Lord is coming up daily with a
smaller figure. He struggles valiantly for a philosophical
attitude. The American humorist Don Herold, looking on
the shiny side, found a consoling thought: "There's one
thing about baldness, it's neat." Another resigned himself:
"Better a bald head than none at all." Shakespeare (who
ought to have been gratified by his bare top since on him it
looked very elegant) kept harking back to the subject and
did some positive, if unreliable thinking: "What he hath
scanted men in hair, he hath given them in wit." Lack of
hair may be a sign of other manly virtues but we have no
reason to think that wit is one of them. And Shakespeare's
comedies probably have nothing at all to do with the
quantity of his hair.

Mankind has had plenty of time to reconcile himself to
his shedding hair. Prehistoric man suffered from baldness.
At least, he had it. We don't know whether he suffered.
He might, like present-day endocrinologists, have seen it
as a good omen. But from the beginning of *recorded* history, baldness has certainly bothered him. In 4000 B.C. it
bothered King Chatos of Egypt's mother, who set out to
cure his with a concoction of dogs' paws, dates, and asses'
hooves.

By 400 B.C., Hippocrates leaned toward a salve of
opium, roses or lilies, wine, and unripe olive oil. His basic
recipe of a resinous compound with alcohol and perfume is
very 1970s balsamy. For more serious cases (including his
own?) he added pigeon droppings and horse radish, which
so far as is known have not been included in today's bal-
sam hair remedies.

The use of bear grease began in Rome and ended in
America around the turn of the present century when

bears (pronounced "bars") were harder to come by and Vaseline was substituted. Many Romans simply painted the hair back on. Octopus fat was also highly regarded by the Romans, and, at least, sounds better than feces and honey, another recommended remedy. One Roman physician prescribed boiled snakes caught at the full of the moon. The American medicine man spiked his snake oil with alcohol, giving one the option of massaging or imbibing. But the most horrible treatment of all was supposed to have been used for the thinning hair of a woman, Diane dePoitiers, mistress of the French Henry II. It called for "the blood of a new-born baby."

By the middle of the eighteenth century, everything was up to date and the big thing was electricity. Unfortunately, a man named Bartlett had the embarrassment, just after publication of his sure-fire electrical system for preserving hair and living to be two hundred, of himself dying at forty completely bald.

Just as medicine today ignores nutrition because faddists have given it a bad name, physicians, sensitive about their own barbering past, ignored hair problems. But when, at the end of the nineteenth century, medical science finally discovered hair and D. Brown-Séquart prescribed sugared female urine, the science of tricology didn't sound like much improvement over Hippocrates and his pigeon droppings. (Lewis Carroll's lobster also sugared his hair but apparently not for medicinal purposes.)

But who goes bald, anyway? Or, better yet, who doesn't? Well, most of the world doesn't as a matter of fact, or at least comparatively rarely: Orientals, blacks (although James Earl Jones, the actor, shaves his head), Indians, Eskimos, the lower primates, and even men of European stock whose male ancestors had hair that stayed put. And, oh, yes. Women and eunuchs.

For those who lack ancestors with firmly attached tops, the most sensible and scientific reaction (if feelings went by facts) on the morning a man knows himself to be balding, would be to announce smugly in Bar Mitzvah-like tone, "Today I am indeed a man," for one of the causes of baldness is a lush supply of male hormones.

Hormones can cause baldness, however, only with the permission of heredity, and how heredity works nobody knows for sure. Research suggests the inherited shape of the head has something to do with it for it is known that a tight scalp is bad and the shape of the head may pull the scalp tight. One experimenter tightened up the scalps of a bunch of monkeys and the tight scalps resulted in baldness. Germans are particularly prone to baldness and are stereotyped as square heads. Fatheads tend to keep their hair a little better, and the fattest parts of the head (around the ears and back) usually hold out longest.

So the best advice is to keep one's scalp loose (and fat) and develop a sober attitude toward life! For a pair of psychiatrists by the names of Szasz and Robertson say laughter is very bad for the hair. It pulls the scalp tight and interferes with the blood supply to the roots. But other theories say that worry and stress are bad, so you can't safely be gloomy either. Maybe Yoga and utter calm are the answer, there not being much you can do about the shape of your head—although other civilizations have. Nurses of the early Greeks bandaged heads to the fashion of their day and region. The Macroenes of Pontus favored a tall shape as a mark of gentility, giving us the word "macrocephalic" (meaning an abnormally large head). The

Scythians preferred a sugar loaf shape, while the classic Greeks found the globular head more beautiful. Poor Pericles, in spite of the Golden Age he bestowed on Greece, had the wrong head (shaped like a mallet) which got him nicknamed old dog head, although even name-calling sounds classical in Greek: cynocephalus.

American men with brush cuts would have felt at home in Signorus, Egypt, or among the low Dutch who all fancied flat-toppped children. The Peruvians liked theirs long and the Moscovites did their best to make their infants' heads broad and noble. When the French aristocracy was sporting enormously tall and ornamental wigs, with or without birdcages perched in them, and it seemed the French aristocracy would go on forever (and forever wear fancier and fancier wigs), midwives were urged to mold female infant heads to shapes best suited to retain the lavish creations. In Old Port in the West Indies, they went so far as to box infants' heads in to make them square.

But to get back to baldness: Aristotle thought sexual intercourse caused baldness. Rabelais thought there was a relationship between virility and baldness (endocrinologists think so too). Hippocrates noticed that eunuchs don't go bald. But modern scientists have found that male hormone injections make *some* of them lose their hair.

Yet, confusingly, baldness-prone European types don't seem to be more virile than other ethnic types. Popular belief, in fact, ascribes that superiority to peoples who rarely go bald and are also short on he-man hair on the chest and face. (One of the stereotypes of the black male is super-virility.)

A man's virility, however, is very susceptible to self-fulfilling prophecies. Therefore, if a man thinks baldness is an indication of age and declining powers, his powers may wane. If, on the other hand, be believes it a mark of superior capacity, it probably is for him.

Neither is holiness necessarily good for the hair. In fact, the case of the prophet Elisha raises a number of theological and psychoanalytic questions. As this irascible man (who invented artificial respiration) was going down the road past Bethel, a group of children ran after him, screaming, "Go down thou Bald Pate." Whereupon, bears came out of the woods and ate forty-two of them. While one sympathizes with the Divine exasperation at such little hoodlums, the punishment seems excessive, as if revealing an abnormal touchiness on the subject of hair loss. Surely a sound spanking, or a sending off to bed without supper, or one hundred lines of "I will never scream at bald prophets again" would have sufficed. After all, they didn't even mug the good man, as New York youths are wont to do without the appearance of even one avenging bear. Which brings us to this theological question: When man was made in the image of his Maker, was he made with hair?

While baldness from Divine, or more earthly, inheritance still lacks a reliable cure, a good many men have taken the sting out of this flaw, and some have been smart enough to turn it into an asset. Yul Brynner, for example, carries his shaved head with such assurance and male arrogance that you never doubt, as you watch him on the screen, that he has chosen a bare head and isn't naturally bald at all. (Is he? I don't know.) Telly Savalas, the television star, does equally well with a completely naked dome and less handsome features.

There have been at least two Golden Ages when balding men looked just fine—adventurous, prosperous, and pleasing to the eye—chiefly because they, their tailors, or their barbers knew exactly how to incorporate the lack of hair into a handsome male image. Shakespeare, for example, did it magnificently. With his ruff and neat Vandyke, Shakespeare's spare top balanced out elegantly. The Elizabethan male was so eye-catching in costume and beard that he didn't really need the extra top trimming.

While the beginning of the twentieth century lacked the advantages of ruff and pirated brocade, it was also a fine time in which to be bald, at least if one had taste or were rich enough to have a good barber. The many styles of moustaches and beards made it easy to ignore baldness in a generally pleasing pattern of hair.

The solid burghers looking out from the pages of *King's Notable New Yorkers of 1896 to 1899* are a handsome lot on the whole, obviously pleased with themselves, their barbers, and that station in life to which it hath pleased the Lord to call them. To think of the august brow of August Belmont, banker and father of the Belmont Racetrack, as a matter of baldness is lèse majesté. A high hairline only elevates the brow and, accordingly, it's noble. A fashionable phrenologist would have been equally pleased with the brows of those two famous restauranteurs, Delmonico (of the steaks) and Louis Sherry (currently memorialized in the freezer of your nearest supermarket), the former looking very British-royalty and the latter looking very writer-philosopher.

And then there is Frederick Law Olmstead with hair as gracefully landscaped and as natural-looking as his Central Park; and two Colgates, James Booman of the university and Samuel of the toothpaste. Samuel really *believed* in cleanliness of skin and teeth—and morals, being president of the New York Society for the Suppression of Vice.

He is tactfully separated from Stanford White by many pages. Whether or not White deserved his fate at the hands of a jealous husband, his barber certainly deserved to be shot. That White managed to be a dangerous seducer of beautiful showgirls in spite of the worst a barber could do seems a clear triumph of sin over adversity. Unlike Olmstead, no professional creativity and art reflected itself in his tonsorial state. His close-cropped, square head quarrels with his soup strainer moustache. Before they could make the movie *The Girl in the Red Velvet Swing*, the story of beautiful Evelyn Nesbitt, her seducer Stanford White, and her crazy-jealous husband Harry Thaw, who shot White, they had to revise history by lengthening White's haircut and trimming his moustache to make the whole enterprise seem worthwhile.

The founders of New York's old, great department stores are a solid relief after such scandalous goings on: James Constable, listed under Dry Goods, only a little balding at the temples, and *very* handsome; Isidor Straus (Macy's, and Abraham and Strauss), with hair almost as bad as Stanford White's (perhaps the same barber?). What little hair he had was gray, cropped very short (must have been very cold that night on the *Titanic*), and completely overpowered by a villainous black beard. But it was a very good head indeed, having an even more remarkable effect on a woman than did Stanford White's, for it was loved enough that one, his wife, chose to go to her death with him on the *Titanic* rather than let him go alone.

Whatever lacks there may have been in Mr. Straus' appearance were more than compensated by his handsome senior partner, Abraham Abraham of A and S, whose thinning hair complemented his dark, poetic eyes with a noble brow.

The period from 1914 to 1960 could hardly have been worse for the bald man. The safety razor had deprived him of the decorative possibilities of beard and moustache, men's styles in clothing left him even fewer, and haircuts had been thoroughly regimented (literally, in two world wars). Baldness, when it came, had a terrible conspicuousness. The bald man could do nothing except comb the remaining hair as deceptively as possible, often making a public announcement thereby of his unhappiness with a status that refused to stay quo. When the assorted Beatle, hippie, and far-out haircuts of the youth cult began to filter through to their elders in the sixties, it again became possible for a balding man with taste, courage, and a good barber to look extremely well. (Although an Elizabethan ruff would still be handy.)

Many people have had baldness thrust upon them, including the patrons of a New York patriotic barber who expressed his Revolutionary sentiments by half shaving his Tory customers and sending them away looking ridiculous.

Many people have lost their hair completely in an attempt to improve it. Ovid scolded one Roman lady for using potions and dyes that made her hair fall out. In one of history's many examples of conquerors conquered by their victims, the Romans aspired to the blond hair of their captives, and much dyeing and bleaching went on, very little of which would have passed any pure food and drugs law. Queen Elizabeth I of England also lost her hair in an attempt to ward off all evidence of aging, and had to resort to wigs, their violent, youthful red making a travesty of her ravaged old face.

We can't be absolutely sure women are not doing similar damage to their hair now. They seem to be going bald today more often than they ever have. Whether this is due to hair preparations, change in diet, air pollution, or the sheer frustration of modern living, no one yet knows.

Of course, women are not immune to the symbolic head shave. The women of some Jewish sects lose it to announce they're married and out of the running. Some African ladies do it to proclaim that they're *not* married and very much *in* the running. (While on the subject of women, if you need to take away the power of a witch, shave her head. She can't do a thing without her hair. So apparently hair is the root of all evil.)

And the ladies of the French aristocracy who escaped the guillotine proclaimed their solidarity with those who didn't by shaving the backs of their heads in the customary pattern used to facilitate the knife.

All this is wound-salting to the poor man of European stock with his here-today-maybe-gone-tomorrow hair who has to watch women and other men swanking around in foliage so securely rooted they can afford to play shaving games, pretending to be bald, left, right, or center as the tribal fancy dictates. Africans, Prussians, and Junkers have sometimes liked all-over jobs; some tribes of Indians fancied back-to-front swaths; Orientals were more inclined to a tiny island topknot in a sea of bare scalp. The Flemish ladies gazing with utter tranquillity from the paintings of Roger Van der Weyden achieved this look by the distinctly untranquil process of pulling out their front hair so that only a high tranquil forehead would show beneath their tranquil linen coifs.

The absurdity of what humanity has done to its own head almost makes one prefer a bare top. Heads are shaved, partially shaved in shapes like privet hedges, and dyed all colors from Mohammet red to Early Briton blue. The Britons also wore long drooping moustaches dyed green and blue. The Black Prince perpetuated the long dangling moustache, dangling in this case through the visor of his helmet, not quite what ladies have in mind when they long for a knight in shining armor. He did have the restraint not to dye it blue.

Even in the cutting of hair, esthetic atrocities abound, as in the bowl haircut of Henry V of England and Shakespeare. The acid test of an actor is whether he can put on a Henry V wig and rise above it. Sir Laurence Olivier achieved triumphs of character-portrayal in his Henry V, probably in a valiant effort to keep the viewers' minds off his haircut. Even the brush-cut cannot compete in ugliness, but when Haldeman, President Nixon's assistant, ran afoul of the law, it was noted that he let his brush top grow along more graceful lines, perhaps for fear a jury might be tempted to convict him on his hair style alone.

Every hirsute monstrosity has looked beautiful to somebody. Every graceful line has looked ugly to somebody else. By the time this book is read, the Henry V bowl haircut may be the fashion and men who aren't wearing it will seem unattractive.

The nonsense and controversy over beards and moustaches has been at least as lively as that over hair. The Persians once fought the Tatars to make them grow Persian style beards. The Tatars in turn made the Chinese adopt the pigtail. Many Chinese preferred to lose their heads. The Revolution of 1911 made them give it up. Again some Chinese preferred to die. Early conquerors of Britain demanded British beards in submission. King Arthur held on to his and fought. In Naples during the French Revolution it was dangerous not to display a queue, short hair being suspiciously revolutionary. And South American revolutionaries and their North American sympathizers have often worn beards in imitation of Fidel Castro.

When Richard Wagner cut his hair to relieve his severe headaches, the barber expected to make a great deal of money. But Frau Wagner beat him to the draw and gathered up the fallen locks for her own enterprises. The barber was cheered, however, when Cosima told the distressed man that the butcher's hair was much like her husband's. Presumably, numbers of adoring young ladies found themselves sighing over treasured mementoes of the butcher.

Chopin, apparently sloppier as a young man than the dandified figure he later cut, succumbed to fashion finally, but (or so he wrote his parents) shaved on only one side because audiences would only be seeing one side of him.

When Spohn, the great violinist, and his pupils called in a barber to shave them all, the barber somewhat apprehensively decided that they all belonged to a secret society. Why else a red brand mark under everyone's left chin?

So lose your hair if you must, but for goodness sake keep your head. Remember, everything that man and nature have been able to do to hair has been considered beautiful. If it's dark or light, blue or purple, it's been fashionable. If it's completely bare or denuded in almost any pattern, it's been fashionable. Completely flat with varnish or bushel basket Afro, shingled, Dutch cut, frizzed, hung over the eyes à la sheepdog, totally invisible, trailing on the ground, or mowed like a lawn, it's all been fashionable and, therefore, beautiful in the eye of the be-holder.

In any case, whatever you've got or haven't got on top, fashionable or not, somebody, somewhere is making one just like it part of a harmonious and desirable image.

As for the impact of bald heads on the opposite sex, don't worry. Balding heads may not always get admired by women but look how often they get loved. (I am in-formed that bald spots can be excellent for kissing.) As for woman with thinning hair, was not Cleopatra bald? And a man may even find a "noble bulge" of intellect under the departing hair.

If you can't take so sane an attitude toward your depre-ciating scalp, you can join plenty of crazy, if famous, com-pany on the subject, although you probably won't have to eat a neighbor to give you courage for a haircut, or require the barber to sneak up on you while you're asleep, or in-stall lightning rods, or demand snakes boiled in the full of the moon.

And there have been those worse off. Once there were people who had hair but no heads, just facial features on the chest, that is, if you believe Pliny, Sir Walter Raleigh, and St. Augustine (who preached to them).

Great Sights—
Near, Far,
and Fuzzy

*I*F THERE'D BEEN A good optometrist at Bunker Hill, maybe the colonials would have won that battle. He might have dissuaded the commanding officer from his colorful, memorable, but extremely short-sighted command. Any eye specialist could have told him what would happen. When some research-minded wag decided to reenact the battle and instructed his "colonials" to "fire when you see the whites of their eyes," the most farsighted were popping off while the nearsighted couldn't tell one enemy from another let alone see the whites of their eyes.

But the battle could have been worse. If the platoon had been made up of famous personages (who often had terrible eyesight), the British might still be running the country. And if his enemy had been Napoleon, the poor colonial would have been in a real quandary. For Napoleon had no whites of his eyes—only lemon yellows.

The people who collect famous spectacles supply us with a variety of insights. First, if you're demanding farsighted leaders, forget it. Better nearsighted. They, on the whole, have done much better, although Martin Luther and Von Hindenburg were farsighted (+3.0 and +4.0 diopters). George Washington was nearsighted. Bismarck was nearsighted (−3 diopters). And as for the Medici, some of them literally couldn't see their hands in front of their faces without their glasses. That's why they became merchants and politicians instead of warriors. The second son of Lorenzo the Magnificent, Giovanni Medici, who eventually became Pope Leo (and had a lot of trouble with a farsighted Augustinian monk named Luther), had lenses that measured −12. diopters. If he had been sitting across the breakfast table from Isadora Duncan, he really wouldn't have been able to recognize her. (A complaint she made about her lover Gordon Craig.)

Unlike the Medicis, Theodore Roosevelt was not discouraged from warfare by his very poor vision, but when warfaring, he did take extraordinary precautions. Before he rode up San Juan Hill, he stuffed every pocket with spare glasses in metal cases (contemporary accounts said twelve pair), in case the first ones should get shot off. His vision, which had been poor all his life, received another blow (this time, literally) while he was in the White House. An over-eager boxing partner, a young captain, forgot to pull his punches and slugged his commander-in-chief. The consequences of this blow were very serious, causing a detachment of the retina which left the eye almost totally blind. The intrepid T.R., who rarely showed any common sense in such matters, was sufficiently alarmed that he refrained thereafter from boxing—and took up jujitsu.

Sometimes nearsightedness has had its compensations. It enabled Samuel Johnson to see his plump, not very attractive, much older wife as beautiful.

History is full of nearsighted people and we have this list of Germans whose spectacles have faithfully been preserved:

	Diopters
Schiller	−2.75
Beethoven	−4.
Mendel	−4.5
Goethe	−6.

If you wish to avoid being nearsighted, pick your ethnic or racial group with care. The more civilized your ancestors, the shorter your sight. For example, if you are an East Indian, it's good for your eyes not to be a Brahmin. They are on the average nearer-sighted than non-Brahmins. The Western nations, not having been civilized too long, are predominantly farsighted (50 percent farsighted to 15 to 20 percent nearsighted), while the Chinese and Japanese, on the other hand, are four times as likely to be nearsighted. Jews and Egyptians, with their ancient civilizations, are also nearsighted.

The explanation is probably very simple. Picture yourself as a nearsighted caveman who can't make out game, dinosaur, or human enemy soon enough. Only under civilized conditions can the nearsighted survive and pass on their nearsighted genes.

Whether your eyes are near- or farsighted may do much to determine the kind of person you will be, according to some theories. While glasses now give near equality of vision, eye defects often go unnoticed in the very young when personalities and habit patterns are being firmly established. To the farsighted child, the world beyond its crib is clear and sharp, the pictures on the nursery wall meaningful and fun, the face in the doorway easily recognized. When older, it runs and plays ball and competes happily and with a feeling of security, while the picture books and drawings, and close play with small toys are blurry or straining to the eyes. The nearsighted baby lives in a much smaller environment. The world outside his window is fuzzy, and he can't run as safely. On the other hand, the up-close world is safe and intriguing and easily mastered. So, it is suggested, does the division between the athlete and the bookworm begin.

Teddy Roosevelt, in addition to being a sickly, asthmatic child, and homely with big protruding teeth, was laughed at for his clumsiness. Even in that wealthy household with much attention to the welfare of its children, no one realized that the boy was clumsy because the world was only a blur to him. Not until age thirteen, when he was considered old enough to use a gun and his father undertook to teach him to shoot, was it discovered that he really could not see.

It might have comforted all the children who through the ages have been scolded for ruining their eyes with books and fine work held too close to know that nearsightedness is born not made and does not result from close work, television, or anything else but the natural shape of the eyeball. The child was too close to the book and spending too much time with it because he could not deal easily with the rest of the world or see the words on the page or the pictures on the television screen unless his nose were almost pressed against them. (While TV won't make him nearsighted, alarmists say color sets may make him a bit radioactive, if he spends too much time too close.) But the Anglo-Saxons had recipes, at least for the poor vision of old age: . . . "then shall he wake up his eye with rubbing, with walking, with ridings either so that a man bear him or convey him in a wain [the age-old admonition, "You should get out more"]. And they shall use little and careful meats and comb their heads and drink wormwood before they take food. Then shall a salve be brought for unsharpsighted eyes: take pepper and beat it and beetle nut and somewhat of salt and wine and that will be a good salve."

By 1299, in Italy, you could forget about pepper and salt salves and try lenses, although if you were Chinese you'd have had them long before—with fashionable tortoise shell frames. The Chinese treated glasses with almost religious veneration and they were worn not only to restore vision but also to bring good luck and high social status, especially if they were rimless. The lenses were ground with sand from the sacred rivers and made of "good fortune" stones: amethyst, rock crystal, and topaz.

The earliest reference in Europe—in the *Trettato del Gorcino da Sandradi Pipozzode Sandero Fiorentino*—is 1299. It tells of a gentleman whose eyes were blurred with age so that he was forced to wear those "glasses they call spectacles, lately invented for the great advantage of old men when their sight grows dim."

Back in the beginning, spectacles had seemed like models of modern science and invention, and numerous celebrated men wore them when they had their portraits painted.

Sir Thomas More (the man for all seasons) wore spectacles for his portrait by Hans Holbein, which must have been before 1535, in which year Sir Thomas was beheaded in the Tower of London for refusing to knuckle under on a matter of church doctrine to his old friend Henry VIII, who had ten pairs of the newfangled spectacles bought for the unprincely sum of 4d apiece. Henry's small jester, Will Somers, had his spectacles riveted into the helmet of his suit of armor.

In El Greco's chilling portrait of Cardinal Inquisitor Nino de Gevara, the cardinal's spectacles arc fastened around his ears with cord just as the Chinese had long worn theirs. The earliest spectacles still preserved belonged to King Augustus Adolphus of Germany. There is also a portrait by Jan Van Eyck of Augustus Adolphus wearing them.

But in 1679 Madrid, the Spanish court wore spectacles as often to gain dignity as to see. (The Marchioness de la Rosa mentions them in the *Ingenious and Diverting Letters of a Lady.*) The English writer Oliver Goldsmith also refers to spectacles for appearance's sake. "Blindness was of late," he said, "become fashionable."

Any nearsighted person who remembers seeing the world for the first time in all its intricacy of detail and richness of coloring, must feel the veneration that the Chinese, and John Bunyan, felt for spectacles. Bunyan once wrote a poem "Upon a Pair of Spectacles," and called them a miracle. And whatever the faults that merited the engraving "May God Forgive Him For His Sins" on the tombstone of Salvino d'Armato, who lived in Firenze, Italy, in the thirteenth century and invented eyeglasses, all nearsighted people would gladly intercede for him at the bar of justice in gratitude for the new world he bestowed upon them. And we'd much rather have him for a patron saint than the one we've got; a rather silly lady by the name of St. Lucy, who in her remorse at looking lustfully at a man, plucked out both her eyes. God apparently couldn't stand such foolishness and gave her a set of re-placements. (There is an affecting picture of her with the new orbs staring up at her from a saucer.) Presumably, the new ones stayed modestly lowered. But this episode got her promoted to patron saint of ophthalmology. Inciden-tally, if you should go into a state of ecstasy, what you've got, ophthalmologically speaking, is a gross divergent squint.

In the manner most highly approved by modern psy-chologists, Lord Nelson was usually His Own Best Friend. When ill, he said, in effect, "There, there. There'll be a battle soon and you'll forget all about it." The loss of his eye, however, shook him badly: "My eye-sight frets me most dreadfully."

But worried or not, he made audacious use of his blind eye at the Battle of Copenhagen. When the flagship's sig-nal to leave off action had been reported by his officer on watch, Nelson took the man's telescope, put it to his blind eye, said, "I really do not see the signal," and continued the fight.

While John Bunyan might think spectacles a miracle, and the Chinese regard them as enhancing of social stand-ing, the ages have not always agreed. Poets Dorothy Parker and Ogden Nash certainly saw them as amatory obstacles, Miss Parker stating categorically that the girl who wore them would have no occasion to fend off male advances (a very blind assumption according to multitudes of ladies in a position to know). Her opinion followed the same vein as the old French couplet:

> *Bonjour lunettes*
> *Adieu fillettes*
> (or)
> Hello glasses
> Goodbye girls

Ogden Nash, while accepting the basic premise, found a silver lining. He pointed out that while the bespectacled lady might not get her neck tacled, she was also less likely to find herself confronted with safety pins and bassinets.

Hitler was too vain to wear glasses and his speeches were always typed out on a large-print "Fuehrer's" typewriter.

In our own era we are naturally going in both directions at once about glasses (as in practically everything else). As at the Spanish court, many people wear spectacles, particularly colored ones, solely for effect, and never have eyeglasses been more elaborately ornamental or more frequently used to complete a sartorial image. (Tinted glasses were worn as far back as 1666 at least, because in that year Samuel Pepys decided to get some green ones for his notoriously poor eyes. The various colors were made then as now for protection from the sun.)

On the other hand, people have sometimes gone through torture to seem not to be wearing glasses at all. One has become accustomed to having one's friends show up looking smug if slightly glazed, or pausing in conversation while they spit out their contacts. And we have envied them their unencumbered visages but remembered that anybody who requires an able-bodied oculist to fight an eyelid open long enough to insert one eye drop may be an unlikely candidate for the intime lens. These optical appurtenances were suggested as far back as 1845 by Sir John Herschel, an astronomer. He suggested they be used only for malformed corneas.

In addition to their cosmetic value and their usefulness to people whose professions or activities preclude conventional spectacles, they have as Sir John anticipated been a godsend to people with certain visual defects that cannot be compensated by regular glasses.

A pair of spectacles over the coat of arms of the Belgian town of Ourdurarde has nothing to do, however, with the invention and early manufacture of glasses, although it's been there for four hundred years at the command of Charles V of Spain. When he paid a ceremonial visit to the town, the townspeople greeted their foreign emperor with less than a royal welcome. He ordered the spectacles erected above the town's crest so that next time they would be able to see him better.

Spectacles might seem miraculous but they have had their limitations, as a 1589 Danish coin points out:

> Of what avail is lens and light
> To one who lacks the mind and might

And there were eye specialists who disapproved of the remedying of physical conditions by mechanical means. In 1583 Dr. Bartesch of Dresden proclaimed: "It is much better and more useful that one leaves spectacles alone. For naturally a person sees and recognizes something better when he has nothing there than when he has something there. It is much better that one should preserve his 2 eyes than that he should have 4."

Goethe hated his glasses and found many reasons for his oft-expressed disapproval, including the moral temptation they presented, not, as one might suppose, of lust but of pride. As he said to an interviewer: "Wearing glasses makes men conceited. Spectacles raise them to a degree of sensual perfection which is far above the power of their own nature but through which the delusion at last creeps in that the artificial eminence is the force of their own nature after all." (I *think* he means you're apt to think you're as good as your bifocals.)

Goethe and other humans might have hated their

glasses but the horse reported in a newspaper on January 13, 1888, had no complaints at all about the spectacles (strength #7) with which a local oculist had fitted him. This equine showed "sedate enjoyment" of the concave lenses fitted for his myopia and whinnied in a "plaintive minor key" when let out to pasture without them (the typical reaction, although somewhat differently voiced, of most myopes deprived of glasses).

The horse was more fortunate than many earlier spectacle-wearers defrauded by racketeers dealing in worthless glasses. By 1670, England had a whole system of fines for selling bad spectacles: £3 for lenses of plain glass in shoddy, easily broken frames. The Vicar of Wakefield's son, like Jack (of Beanstalk notoriety), was a poor bargainer and when sent to town to trade the family horse for provender, returned instead with a gross of green spectacles to be sold at a fabulous profit, and was most distressed to learn that he had been had.

In olden days, if spectacles weren't, as Goethe held, a moral risk, they might very well be a hazard to your eyes because they were fitted almost at random. (Within my lifetime, old people could buy reading glasses in stores, trying on spectacles till they found a pair that suited.) In the beginning, because vision faded with age, spectacles were prescribed according to one's age and were referred to not as weak or strong but as young or old. Since the most-read book in the English-speaking world was the Bible and sales might fall off as customers aged, one company very wisely provided both the Holy Writ and the spectacles to go with it.

The American Founding Fathers were well protected from both chicanery and poor fit by having an expert (in everything) among them. Benjamin Franklin, in some hiatus in his diplomating and tempting of the lightning of the gods, had found time to invent bifocals, which the other Fathers, all younger than old Ben, but still with aging eyes, found very useful. Thomas Jefferson, for example, wore spectacles of the type designed by Franklin.

James Buchanan's problem was more complicated, and he had to keep his head tilted to the side because one eye was placed higher than the other. He also, rather like Hamlet's stepfather with his "one drooping and one mirthful eye," was prepared for all occasions, having one eye that was farsighted and one that was nearsighted. He closed one eye or the other to give sharp vision at whatever distance was required. He read incessantly and never wore glasses till his last year.

Zachary Taylor was very nearsighted and had double vision at all distances. He squinted terribly and had to close one eye in order to read at all. He was also once shortsightedly economical. He missed getting the news that he had been nominated for president because the letter came postage collect, and he refused it.

Abraham Lincoln, like Buchanan, had a lateral imbalance. In his case, the right eye rolled up a trifle (or the left one rolled down), a little like being cross-eyed at a 90-degree angle, up and down instead of cross-wise. (Son Robert was cross-eyed.) In normal health and normal circumstances, Lincoln's eyes compensated very well for this defect.

He later bought glasses, which have been preserved, from a jewelry store in Bloomington, Illinois. Since they were very strong ($-6.$ diopters), maybe two or three times stronger than he needed, they may explain the severe headaches he had when he read fine print.

But what most troubled Lincoln was when he seemed

to see things beyond the scope of any spectacles, as the time he saw looking back at him from the mirror not one face but two—a living countenance and a ghostly counter-part.

On the night before he was to attend a play called *Our American Cousin* at Ford's Theatre he dreamed that he awoke to the sound of people sobbing, and observed funeral arrangements in the White House. He saw a coffin with soldiers guarding it and questioned them about who was dead, and heard them answer, "The President, killed by an assassin."

The visual anomalies of the artist have always been of special interest for the way they may influence his art. At the Ecole des Beaux Arts in Paris, a survey of 128 pupils and masters showed that, unlike the typical Frenchman, who is farsighted, the artists were nearsighted in a ratio of 2 to 1. This, of course, fits in neatly with the notion that nearsighted children are inclined to occupations that can be carried out at short range, within their sharpest vision.

It may be that some impressionists in the past didn't know they were impressionists but were merely painting the way the world looked to them (and presumably to everybody else).

An Italian artist known as Guicino ("The Squinter"; his real name was Giovanni Barbieri) did paintings that were flatly two-dimensional because his two eyes weren't coordinated well enough to give him the extra dimension.

Many other artists suffered from similar misalignment of the two eyes. Albrecht Dürer reveals his problem not only by his style but in his self-portraits. The characteristic tilt of the head and the deviated right eye is notable in his self-portrait of 1493 (now in the Louvre). Whether he grew more truthful as he aged, or the right eye drifted farther from alignment, the disorder apparent in his mature portraits does not appear in the self-portrait of the thirteen-year-old Albrecht. One suspects the young painter's vanity may have outdistanced his integrity as an artist.

Art historians interested in medicine and optics have had a field day with El Greco. The theory has been put forth that El Greco painted long, gaunt figures because of an astigmatism that made him see people that way. (Astigmatism distorts images much as a funhouse mirror does by a change in the curvature of the receiving surface.) It's been a popular and widespread notion and a very interesting idea. The only problem is that the arguments against seem stronger than the arguments for it.

The evidence for: El Greco's figures are elongated and they became more so as the artist grew older. Trevor-Roper, who is an authority on vision and art, states that a slight astigmatism can develop with age and change the proportions in an artist's paintings. He cites Gainsborough as well as El Greco, but he also points out that artists usually compensate for the distortion when drawing. (This is a tricky argument to follow, so watch it!) If, to the astigmatic eye, a person looks taller than he does to the normal eye, so does a normal painting look taller. That is, if the artist drew them elongated to the normal eye, they would look elongated also to his own.

Furthermore, El Greco was much influenced by Byzantine art which has tall flat figures (maybe *those* were the artists with the astigmatism), and Byzantine art was in general vogue in El Greco's day. Also the mannerists in Rome were experimenting with mirrors and visual apparatus and they often did tall figures. To El Greco's school of artists, the desirable length of a body was 9 heads tall. (The standard today is 7½.)

Further, astigmatism does not vary from day to day as El Greco's elongation of figures did. Even within a single painting, some people were and some weren't. But the clincher is X-ray evidence which shows the underlying sketches to be normal and lengthened only to suit his artistic purpose in the finished painting.

But anybody might have come to the same conclusion by noticing that El Greco's saints and Spanish nobles when they laid them down to die were just as over-stretched as when they were standing up; and El Greco presumably didn't tilt his head 90 degrees while he painted them recumbent. If it had all been astigmatism, they should be tall and thin standing up and short and fat lying down.

But if astigmatism is hard to diagnose in an artist's work, near- and farsightedness are often easy. They reveal themselves by two signs in particular: how the artist handles perspective and how large a view he tends to choose. You see, if he does not see too well at a distance, he may use a simple geometric perspective, not realizing this rule does not hold true for more distant vistas. And one can often trace the increasing farsightedness of the artist's middle and old age. Unlike nearsighted artists, whose work may be fuzzy because that's the way the distant vista looks to them, the aging artist's work may lose sharpness because the easel is not in sharp focus. Along with the loss of detail from changing vision, also comes the loss in dexterity which has allowed the meticulous line. These changes are, for example, said to be evident in the later work of Daumier and Piero de la Francesca and, of course, in the work of Michelangelo, whose eyes failed him. But even in the last work of Leonardo da Vinci there are signs that his eyes were changing.

Many impressionist painters had poor eyesight: Derain, Braque, Vlaminck, Segonzac, and Matisse. Degas accommodated to his failing eyesight first by using photographs of models and then by going to sculpture where the sense of touch could still keep his work true.

With the development of glasses, the visually impaired artist then had his two different visual worlds, either of which he could choose to convey—the cold, sharp world of 20-20 vision or the softened line with its ambiguities to be filled in not by the eye but by the imagination.

The fact that television was (and still is sometimes) extremely unclear, has probably profoundly altered our perceptions. We have grown accustomed to its impressionism. We have learned to watch and in our minds turn double images into single ones and ugly distorted images into· beautiful ones, often without much awareness that what we see with our imaginations is not what the eye sees. But psychologists have known for a long time that we often see what ought to be there, or what we wish were there, even if it isn't.

Rhoda Kellogg, a researcher with the stamina to examine 300,000 drawings of preschool English, Chinese, and American children, discovered that they agree on twenty basic scribbles and six basic diagrams. And, strangely—or perhaps quite naturally—these marks and shapes are very like the shapes we see with our eyes closed and the eyeball pressed (or what toddlers see when they bump their heads—the first abstract art experience?). And both the small children's drawings and the "stars" we see when bopped on the head resemble some of the cave drawings of primitive man.

Whether we agree on basic scribbles, we certainly don't all agree on color. If it had been Milton or Goethe who saw that rainbow of Wordsworth's, their hearts probably would not have levitated even slightly. First, because they were less flighty than the renowned Lake poet. But mainly because their rainbows had only three colors, they being somewhat color-blind, hardly worth a single jeté of the aorta. The English landscape artist Constable lived in a similarly muted world.

Much art has been sharply affected by the artist's color vision. Nearsighted people, because of the elongated eyeball, see red objects most clearly. Farsighted people have sharper vision in blue. It has been suggested that the predominantly nearsighted Chinese and Japanese enjoyment of the red end of the spectrum is because of this. (The Japanese have only recently coined a proper word for blue.)

I'm not sure whether anybody has measured the length of the bowerbird's eyeball, but this creature is a living nut for the color blue. He spends days, even weeks, painting his nest blue and furnishing it for his mate in Bowerbird House Beautiful—all matching shades of blue. He will thieve or kidnap or even kill so long as the color is right: shards of broken blue crockery, blue theater tickets, blue rags, blue centipedes, and blue feathers tweaked from the plumage of other birds. If the hold-up victim is too uncooperative in parting with the coveted feather, the bowerbird has been known to murder the victim. His art technique consists of making a brush by rubbing a twig till its end is exposed and feathered, then using it to apply blue paint made from berries. He instantly removes any red objects from the vicinity of the nest (too apt to bring on sexual impulses at inappropriate times).

All of this is perfectly true.

And after all those prenatal influencings, what color are its eggs? A blotchy brownish white, while any old robin pulling worms out of your lawn can produce eggs of a divine blue without any of this arty exhibitionistic hanky-panky.

It may occur to English readers still predominantly far-sighted (short eyeballed) from not having been civilized long enough to have really defective sight, to wonder about the eyeball measurement of their ancestors who stubbornly insisted on painting themselves blue instead of nice warm reds and browns and oranges. And it may be because of their eyeballs that the color of valor in England is blue while the Chinese are brave in red.

Abraham Lincoln never saw the American flag—at least not the red, white, and blue. He'd have had to give three cheers for the dark gray, white, and light gray of Old Glory, because he was almost completely color-blind.

Color vision is one of the compensations for being human. Below the anthropoid apes, few animals have it, so the bowerbird would be remarkable even without its monomania for blue and its artistic bent.

Many famous people in history have had to make do with one eye. The two best-known of our era are probably the entertainer Sammy Davis, Jr., who wears an artificial eye and whose lack would go unnoticed if he did not freely mention it, and General Moishe Dayan, who lost his in battle when he was young and who prefers to wear a patch. The loss does not seem to have interfered with the career of either or with their attractiveness to women. The burly Russian giant, Potemkin, certainly lost none of his sex appeal because of his missing eye. Of all Catherine the Great's lovers, he was the one who endured longest—fifteen years.

And, apparently, the Duc de Bourbon, son-in-law of Louis XIV and little admired on any count, wouldn't have looked a bit better with two eyes. Somebody said nastily that his other eye was so red that it was impossible to distinguish the good from the bad. Louis, however, had not the slightest aversion to bad eyes in general, no matter what he might think of the Duc's. The king's earliest mistress had been a lady with one eye.

The rovingest eye in history belonged to the French hero and patriot Gambetta. For many centuries, it was a custom, fortunately now lost, to pay one's respect to the dead by retaining parts of him as a keepsake. When Gambetta had an injured eye removed at the age of eight or nine, nobody knew he was destined for fame, so the French surgeon merely preserved the specimen and sent it on to a colleague in Germany for his eye collection. But young Gambetta went on to become a great statesman and a public idol, so that when he passed on, his component parts were at a premium, and the gothic practice reached its zenith. One admirer got the heart, another the brain, a third the viscera. And the hue and cry was on for the missing eye. The French doctor communicated with the German doctor who apparently had absentmindedly given it to somebody else and couldn't remember who, and it has never been found and for all we know is still roving. When Sir Walter Raleigh, Rawley, Rolley, or Rawleigh lost his head, Lady Raley, or Ralye (there are at least seventy-five different spellings, nobody in Shakespeare's [or Shapspur's] day having the faintest idea of how to spell his own name) retrieved the head and carried it with her wherever she went as long as she lived.

Shelley's Mary at first balked at this act of wifely devotion. When her drowned poet's stout friend Trelawney rescued the poet's heart from his pyre and carried it off to Mary, Mary merely recoiled, so he gave it to the minor poet (and major pest) Leigh Hunt, who was delighted with the treasured relic. Mary eventually changed her mind and demanded it back. Hunt wasn't parting with it, and there was a nasty brouhaha in literary circles before she pried it away from him, after which she carried it in a silken bag for the rest of her life.

So let's keep track of our eyes, and whether far or near sighted, relax in the good company of fame and wear our spectacles as proudly as the Ancient Chinese and Sir Thomas More. If you happen to be cross sighted (hardly anybody is anymore, because of the skill of eye specialists), you can imagine yourself as a ruler of the Mayans or a Mayan princess with this ultimate mark of royalty and nobility. In fact, if your eyes had not crossed by themselves, they would have dangled objects close to your infant face to promote this badge of superiority.

As for upside-down-sightedness, think nothing of it. We've all got that and are so smart we need neither glasses nor specialists but remedy it all by ourselves. The pictures received by our retinas are wrong side up as on the film of a camera but we aren't even aware of it. By some mental abracadabra we turn them right side up and go blithely on our way.

Sinking Your Teeth Into History

*T*HE ONLY THING worse than a trip to the dentist is having no dentist to make a trip to. Count the cavities yours has nipped in the bud. Then imagine them un-nipped—and that was the mouth that was. For most of the world. In most of the ages. Globally, there is only one dentist for every two and a half million teeth. All primitive man could do was wait for his bad tooth to fall out, knock it out with a rock, or appeal to the gods. Of course, he didn't have as many bad teeth as we do; at least, the Danes in the Stone Age didn't. Only 14 percent of their skulls have tooth decay, a far better record than Crest's. But civilization was terrible for teeth.

Except for our souls (about which there is considerable difference of opinion) our teeth are all that ultimately endure, long after bones have gone to dust. So, it's understandable that teeth should be regarded with awe and endowed with many magical properties. When the Persians were expecting a universal destruction like that which hit Noah, or, rather, hit everybody except Noah and his two by twos, and they were preparing lists of those to be saved, you could be doomed by bad teeth as easily as by those other attributes so offensive to the gods: lunacy, lying, and poverty. Their census-takers, apparently, weren't too thorough, however. Some prevarication genes seem to have sneaked on board. At least, an English traveler in the nineteenth century complained that the Persians were terrible liars.

It can be a good thing, spiritually speaking, to wear necklaces of teeth, particularly your enemies'. Even in contemporary America, the spirits keep up a lively interest in our dentition as shown by regular visits of the Tooth Fairy.

That dentistry itself is of divine origin may be hard for you to credit as you sit spitting in a dental chair. This is not prima facie a religious experience although the words that spring to mind as the drill accelerates may be those uttered, although with somewhat different emphases, in houses of worship.

But divine it was. The first dentures on record were made in India before 5000 B.C. by the twin sons of Asvin, the sun god, for a third-rate deity named Pūshan, the god of nourishment. He lost his first set not, as you might guess, from eating too much rich food but in a fracas at a divinities' picnic.

By 800 B.C. the Etruscans had become knowledgeable dentists, and a mere five hundred years later were doing fancy bridgework.

The Egyptians' phenomenal skill in embalming leaves us plenty of evidence that they were terrible dentists.

Their nobles went into eternity with every luxury including food, but often with very poor teeth to eat it with. But, at least, while Egyptian dentistry couldn't do much for your teeth, your physician could recommend forty-eight different kinds of painkiller.

The ancient Israelites seemed to specialize in ornamentation and made splendid gold teeth. The collection of laws and prescriptions in the Talmud, in the Mishna, deals with such matters because naturally there had to be carefully detailed laws. For example, were they or were they not to be worn on the Sabbath? "A woman may go out with . . . whatever she may be accustomed to keep in her mouth provided she does not put it in her mouth on the Sabbath to commence with; if it fall out of her mouth, she must not replace it. As for a metal or gold tooth, Rabbi permits it but the sages prohibit it." These golden teeth were apparently removable.

Roman law (in 450 B.C.) forbade the removal of gold from a dead body's mouth, thereby imposing a hardship not only on ghouls but also on hardworking husbands whose wives expired too suddenly to remove the family gold reserves and leave them behind.

The ancient civilizations of Ecuador and Mexico were even fancier than the Israelites' and the Romans'. They inlaid gems and other minerals and must have looked very sparkly.

The Greeks, at least, had giant-size extractors, because a sample hangs in the Temple of Apollo at Delphi. It seems that mice and sun gods and teeth go together in dental folklore all over the world. In parts of Greece, Apollo was the Mouse God, and mice had lots of theological clout, particularly over teeth. For example, for toothache (or bad breath) you take the head of one hare, and three mice; burn these to ashes (the liver and kidney should be done separately). Mix with equal parts of marble dust and, if to be used as a mouth wash, mix with water.

Despite their formidable tooth extractor, the Greeks were reluctant to pull teeth at all, until they were almost ready to fall out of their own volition, so much mouse dust was probably required to ease the pain. The Egyptians preferred fresh mouse applied to the cheek.

The Japanese were less conservative than the Greeks about tooth removal; they did it with their bare hands, although not, as one might fear, with a karate chop. They diligently practiced extracting pegs from wood of increasing hardness, until finally they had the strength and finesse to tackle molars.

The Chinese did not need the Indians' array of dental instruments, forty-eight Egyptian painkillers, or well-exercised Japanese-style finger muscles. They used acupuncture. They also decorated their teeth with gold, for Marco Polo mentions both men and women of Kardendon, on the border of Burma, sporting well-fitting jackets of ornamental gold over their teeth. It should, of course, be noted that one of the safer places to keep your money is in your teeth.

The Arabians applied melted butter with wool as a tooth remedy. They also borrowed the complex methods and instrument design of neighboring India. Abulcasis, tenth-century physician and surgeon to the caliph, wrote a manual of surgery so valuable that it was published in Europe for centuries. Cascellius, a Roman senator, was the first dentist specifically recorded as being a dentist.

False teeth in Rome, as everywhere else since, occasionally gave trouble. A witch running away lost hers in her hurry. (General Grant's orderly threw his into the river with a basin of water, and the general had to send north for his dentist.) The Latin poet Martial, who tells us of the witch in haste, brought up other oral matters. To a lady who had evidently offended his poet's soul, he wrote the lines: "Without shame you make show with bought teeth and hair." To another, he proffers distinctly unsoulful advice: "That your breath or your mouth may not smell from yesterday's wine, use you the pastilles of Cosmus." To a third: "How do I explain that your kiss smells of myrrh?"

To avoid such problems, the Japanese made tooth brushes by fringing the end of twigs and used tooth powder. Bad breath has always been a worry, and, despite the glowing optimism of mouthwash commercials, is still not completely under control, but of course, nowhere near as troublesome as it was to Dr. Codman, distinguished dental practitioner, addressing the American Dental Academy in 1879:

"Everything that disturbs the digestion either from internal or external causes will prevent the cure of this disease. Want of exercise, too much worry, or mental strain, too much sensuality, all conspire," he continued in a flight of metaphor, "to prevent the physiological fires from consuming the fuel without smoke." Then the speaker turned to a most embarrassing professional problem—the dentist with bad breath: "What palliative shall the dentist have who bending over the patient discovers that there is an unpleasant taint to his breath? The first thing he must do is to close his mouth tightly and breathe through his nose. Have at hand some disinfectant and every chance he can get make for the remedies, rinse the mouth rapidly, and silently run back to the patient and keep his mouth closed."

Failing these amelioratives, the poor halitositic could call upon St. Cosmus, the patron saint of dentists. To insure that your saint should have no conflict of interest, dentists have one saint, their patients another—St. Appolinera, a martyr because of the unpleasant experience of having her teeth knocked out.

What prayers or incantations one says over one's cavities may depend on what one thinks caused the trouble. Babylonian charms and spells were addressed to casting out invading worms. The Babylonians, among many others, held to the worm theory of dental decay, an essentially sound hypothesis, although by the time William Hunter solved this particular whodunit in 1901, the living organisms eating our cavities in their sugar-intoxicated mania were found to be many thousand times smaller than the Babylonians envisaged.

The Saxons gave scope for learned controversy by evolving *two* theories: tooth decay might be caused by worms, but was more probably a corrosive moisture from the brain—a kind of postcerebral drip. If some historical rumors are true, the Saxons didn't have cavities themselves because of their well-balanced diets.

Their early English counterparts were not so fortunate, nor were they fortunate in their dentists. Their tooth-pullers were largely scum de la scum, although part of this may be calumny since people have always had negative attitudes about fellow human beings who insert instruments of torture. But deserving or not, English dentists were placed in the same social stratum as thieves and other scoundrels. This at least freed the patient from am-

bivalence. Your dentist in those days probably richly deserved your animosity. Today when not playing Marquis
de Sade, he is likely to be a kindly pillar of society, one's
equal in gentility, and a good deal one's superior in pelf.
If, acting under the prodding of one's lawless unconscious,
one breached the canons of propriety and actually bit the
hand that drilled, one might be overcome with shame and
remorse. This point was unintentionally verified by the
author, who, mouth deadened, did not detect the presence
of a digit among assorted bales of cotton, and chomped.
While on the whole regretful of this unseemly incident, it
has, upon later seating in the dental chair, returned as a
semibeautiful memory.

In Merrie Olde Englande, no qualms need have as-
sailed one except those concerned with longevity, since
your friendly neighborhood tooth-drawer might also be
the local cutthroat. You could of course try other Old English methods of making a tooth fall out, like cauterizing it
or rubbing your gums with fat from a frog.

The first welfare dentist on record was Matthew Flint,
ordered in 1400 to be paid 6d daily at the City of London
Exchange to perform dental work for those who could not
pay.

But with the Barbers' Charter of Incorporation, which
included tooth-pulling as one of their legitimate functions,
dentists had their feet on the somewhat grubby first rung
to their present enviable share of the gross national product.

But the real father of modern dentistry was Pierre Fou-
chart. He was *chirurgien dentiste* to the bumpkin
Louis XV, and thus escaped the glorious Sun King, Louis
XIV, with his notably inglorious teeth. The magnificent
Louis had arrived in the world with two teeth in good

working condition, which made the royal infant unpopular with wet nurses, who often retired from his service with battle scars. He became king before he was five, a sad little pawn of power politics with a powerful and exceedingly stingy guardian, Cardinal Mazarin. The king's small toes sometimes poked through the palace's ragged sheets. Petit Louis was sometimes whisked out of even this ragged shelter in the middle of the night and rattled over wintery roads (once below zero) to save him from insurrectionists. And the child had terrible toothaches. Later, when about to be married, he had all his upper left teeth removed in an operation so unfortunate it made an opening through his jaw to his nose, and left the dentist even more prostrated than the the royal patient.

His bride did little to improve the family tooth situation. Her teeth were black and poor Maria-Theresa was also "without beauty or brains."

If Gautama Buddha, owner of the most famous tooth in history, had been toothless, his country would have benefited enormously, for his followers fought one another like maniacs, war after war, for possession of that most sacred relic, the tooth of Buddha. It was, after being dragged back and forth through the centuries and over the map of India, finally carried off to Ceylon. When the Portuguese occupied Ceylon in the 1500s, they seized the tooth, burned it to dust, scattered the dust to the winds and thought they had ended the hassle once and for all. But the khan replied by making an ivory replica twenty times life-size and building a palace, the Dalaca Malagravia, for Buddha's new denture.

Like Louis XIV, Queen Elizabeth I suffered with toothaches all her life. She had black teeth from too much sugar. By the age of three, not only was the child deep in trouble for being the daughter of the recently beheaded Anne Boleyn (whose name Elizabeth never spoke in her whole life), but she had "great pain with her great teeth and they come very slowly forth," wrote her worried guardian, adding that because the child was in pain she could not be adequately controlled. The princess was apparently treating her protector to early samples of the famous Tudor temper.

When she was forty-five, her toothaches were still a problem to her protectors. The Privy Council in its desperation went so far as to consult a foreigner, a terrible risk because foreigners might turn out to be Jews or even Roman Catholics, but the Council was beside itself. The doctors disputed furiously. The queen must have the tooth pulled. Elizabeth was terrified. Finally, Bishop Aylmer of London solved the dilemma. Like a mother demonstrating that spinach tastes good, the bishop explained reassuringly that he had had many teeth pulled; it hardly hurt at all, look—whereupon, he had the tooth-puller extract one of the bishop's own that she might observe for herself. So reassured, Elizabeth gathered her courage to the sticking point and the tooth came out.

She'd never have understood a man like Hitler, who had his lower front teeth removed and replaced with a bridge merely because the spit collected and sputtered his oratory. But if Elizabeth had bad teeth it probably wasn't for lack of taking care of them. She had many choices of popular dentifrices: powdered burnt honey and salt; powdered rabbit's head; pomegranate peel; pumice, brick, and coral to remove stubborn stains—also, probably, enamel—and sublimate of mercury. She had applicators, including a gift of "4 tooth cloths of Coarse Holland wrought with black silk and edged with bone lace." And she heeded the

admonition "never pick with an iron toothpick," but being
a queen could not use the lowly, if highly recommended,
wood pick. She had to settle for gold. (She also had a gold
earpick.) Toothpicks also made first-rate gifts, thoughtful
and not too personal. The one Philip of Bavaria received
from Lady Lisle was indeed a cherished memento. The
donor had used it herself for seven years before passing it
on to Philip. (In our day, we lack such thoughtfulness,
and toothpicks are worthy of mention only because they
are the foreign body surgeons most often retrieve from our
interiors.)

Failing success with these Elizabethan tooth hygienes,
one could still follow sage advice: "If teeth are badly eaten
away, lacking, or too large, the thing is to lisp and simper
rather than laugh or smile broadly" (Mona Lisa?).

False teeth were beginning to be the thing by the days
of Good Queen Anne. The Duchess of Portland wrote,
"Lord Hervey has the finest set of Egyptian pebble teeth
[agate] you ever saw."

What dentist made Lord Hervey's elegant teeth we do
not know, but we do know about James Spence, dentist to
George III. He preferred to use, not Egyptian pebble, but
human teeth. A gentleman marveled, "as white and polished as ivory, the only wonder was how they came to lose
their destined home and how they were found where I
saw them." How they departed the mouths that grew
them might be quite simple. If you were poor enough,
you sold them. When young Emma Lyon was discharged
from her position as a housemaid for misconduct, she was
so desperate she contemplated selling her teeth. Fortunately for Romance, she decided to make other anatomical
trades instead and continued in a path of misconduct
which led her to Lord Hamilton's nephew, who paid off a

debt to his uncle by giving him Emma, and thence to the love of Horatio Nelson and the immortality of stage, screen, and print.

No doubt teeth were also lifted from the dead, but many synthetic materials were tried. The Duke of Wellington's were probably ivory, although some say human teeth and others say calf. The plate that fitted over the gum was lined with gold, a great refinement and they were held together, as was customary, with mouth-filling springs, altogether an impressive creation worthy of the Iron Duke. He kept them in a silver humidifier with a wet sponge filled with some aromatic, since ivory was known to smell. His dentures carried the number 171145, which has been a perplexing matter to dental historians. What does the number mean? A goldsmith's mark? Not likely, since most dentists did their own goldsmithing. Problems. Problems.

The only surgery Napoleon ever endured in his life was a tooth extraction on the island of St. Helena, his final exile. He rarely took medicine and had little respect for pill dispensers, although he was once overjoyed, and so was everybody else, by a visit from the court physician, Dr. Couvisant. While making his daily rounds of the imperial household in the Tuileries, the good doctor found the emperor in a maniacal rage because of a splinter of toothpick wedged between his teeth.

George Washington's false teeth are almost as widely known, if less revered, than Buddha's real one. Everybody knows he had them and that they didn't fit too well. Some people even think his stern, paternal look was due to his teeth and not his emotions; his teeth might slip if he forgot to look glum. (Actually, he seems to have been a rather amiable man, and he managed to lead one of the few revo-

lutions in history where, once free of the enemy, the revolutionaries did not start killing one another off.) To
achieve even as good a facial expression as we are accustomed to, his portraitists apparently had to cheat a bit.
Gilbert Stuart, in his 1795 picture, had Washington stuff
his cheeks with cotton to plump them out, in order to
compensate for his ill-fitting dentures.

We have it on the authority of the Daughters of the
American Revolution that one of the things everybody
knows about his false teeth doesn't happen to be true. He
never wore wooden ones, although wood couldn't have
been more harrowing than what he did wear. The facial
distortions were caused by his assortment of elephant, hippopotamus, and walrus tusks (his "sea horse teeth"), plus
gold and other metals and the bulky springs that held the
upper and lower dentures together. He often had a swollen and uncomfortable appearance and he looked quite different from day to day depending upon how thoroughly
his mouth was armored. He returned one set because
"they bulge my lips out in such a manner as to make them
considerably swollen." Chewing was miserable—the machinery slipped and the springs cut—and he couldn't have
managed a toothy politician's smile no matter what.

Assorted articles on his teeth in medical, dental, and
historical society journals have been bringing us every
breathless detail beginning in 1839 or earlier. And letters
from Washington to his dentist have been faithfully preserved. He needed, he said in one of them, plaster of Paris
so he could take an impression of his gums for a new set.
He also complained, in 1783, that he was having considerable trouble with his teeth. This news, no doubt, brought
aid and comfort to the enemy, since it was found among

General Howe's papers, having, apparently, been intercepted by the British.

His first letter, in 1781, had gotten through safely. Then, he had needed pincers to tighten the wire on his teeth and scrapers "as my teeth are in need of cleaning." "It would come by post and in return," he added reassuringly (revolutionaries do not necessarily make good credit risks), "the money shall be sent as soon as I have the cost of it."

A biblical proverb declaims: "How sharper than a serpent's tooth to have a thankless child." A thankless *parent* is no prize either. And George Washington's was enough to set his very dentures, wood, ivory, or hippopotamus, on edge. While his new nation idolized its leader, Mother Washington complained incessantly to her son (and to anyone else who would listen) what an ingrate he was; how he kept her in poverty and squalor; how he had forgotten his poor, aged mother now that he was a hero. The old lady went on and on while her great son patiently continued to provide well for her but probably dreaded encounters more than with the Redcoats, or even his warring cabinet.

In 1790, John Greenwood, George Washington's favorite dentist, invented the dentist's foot drill from his grandmother's spinning wheel, but he and his son used it for many years before it became generally available to the profession. In 1829, the coiled flexible wire was added which allows your dentist to drill up, down, and crosswise with such virtuosity.

But nothing is perfect. By 1883, dentists in conclave were sheepishly admitting to the extraction from time to time of the wrong tooth.

In the 1800s came the relief of anesthesia, especially that blessing of the dentist's chair, cocaine.

Lincoln had to bring his own chloroform for a tooth extraction because Washington dentists did not yet have it.

But, probably, Lister's advocacy of cleanliness and sterilized instruments was as important to tooth sufferers as novocaine. And, finally, with antibiotics to protect us from the dangerous and painful gum infections of the past, and fluorides to discourage the rampaging little organisms etching out our cavities, we are again free to concentrate on beautification, as the Mexicans, the Peruvians, and the ancient Israelites did. But fashions change, and we can no longer add a gold cap or insert an emerald or two to brighten our smiles and upgrade our social positions.

Alas, the only beautification permitted us is straightening and whitening—but don't whiten if you're going to Malaya, because the Malays think white teeth are disgusting. Some Malay groups add extra coloring to their teeth by filing patterns and then staining, the filed areas being porous enough to absorb the stain. By this method one can have very natty checked and mottled teeth. Some people in Deaf Smith County, Texas, achieve this without filing because a severe natural excess of fluorides in their water does the job of mottling for them. Some Indonesians, in addition to filing their teeth, insert small brass studs which the movement of the lips keeps always polished and shiny. Some Africans also file their teeth into points and angles.

A Regency buck filed his teeth so he could whistle through them just as shrilly as the coachmen who were his chief companions. This custom of tooth-filing has also been widely practiced by an American tribe of nomads found chiefly in Hollywood and New York but frequently seen as far afield as London, Paris, Rome, Portugal, and Switzerland, roaming in search of food and larger deposits of lucre. This group, called Actors, have many interesting tooth practices, and have been known to remove quite sound teeth in order to replace them with factory substitutes which they have inserted in patterns believed to be more esthetically pleasing than the original. While Lady Hamilton made the movies by not parting with her teeth, others have arrived by doing so. This custom still persists into the modern era although less practiced than in the Great Movie Age, when leading members of the tribe (who, surprisingly, were often women or even small children) might have much dental ornamentation. Even the tiniest gaps between the teeth were considered unacceptable and had to be filled in with a toothlike substance, as with the very small space between the teeth of their most outstanding tribeswoman, Garbo.

It is sometimes feared by young or shy denture-wearers that artificial teeth may pose a barrier to osculation of the more intimate variations now current. But please note that some of the most expert kissing you've ever watched on the movie screen was done by denture-wearers, and there is every evidence that movie stars with china fittings lead active smooching lives off camera as well. In my years as a psychotherapist, I never have encountered a case where false teeth posed a threat to oral togetherness. When you're attracted enough for real sex, or love-making, such details become inconsequential. (Somebody has said that the real test of love, however, is whether you could share a toothbrush.)

The less mixed-up one's ethnic background, probably the less mixed-up one's teeth and the better chance of having the right size teeth for the space allotted to them. A much-conquered people, like the English, for example, often have more crooked teeth than those of less sullied blood. An Englishman risks finding himself with Viking teeth in a Roman jaw, while his once colonial subjects often have beautiful, even, flashing teeth. Between the sugar spoils of pirate and Empire, and the dubious ancestral conglomerates, teeth have never been England's proudest heritage. (Which probably explains why the delicious, hard-crusted breads of France never crossed the English Channel.) In fact, nobody but Queen Victoria seems to have had a good word for British teeth. When her daughter, the crown princess of Germany, was pregnant with Kaiser Wilhelm, Victoria dispatched English dentists to the scene because "German dentists and German teeth are so bad." Not that she generally admired the English, but she did have a kindly word for Americans. "Yankees," she wrote, "should not be abused for their natural defects."

The melting pot of America is, of course, an orthodontist's paradise (57 percent of Harvard students have malocclusions). The skill of these orthodontists in sorting out our oral snafus has made them among the wealthiest of dentists.

Even Roosevelt teeth are probably under control in this generation but they used to be esthetically very unpredictable and young Teddy Roosevelt's were too big, too forward, with too much spacing. Once he could muster a large bushy moustache he covered them completely, or could have if he'd followed the Elizabethan advice and kept his lip more buttoned. But he had a wide-open smile and a hearty bull-moose laugh and the camouflage often proved inadequate. Cousin Eleanor had no such hirsute recourse and even worse teeth, probably the most noted of the twentieth century, since her enemies seemed to feel her appearance validated their grievances. And she had enemies of whom any right-thinking woman might be proud. In Eleanor Roosevelt's childhood, her teeth had been a source of distress and contributed to her shyness and awkwardness, but her handsome cousin Franklin fell in love with her anyway. (He himself had escaped the family tooth problem.) And when she lost his love to another woman, it was because of her nagging and not her teeth.

Now, of course, children need not grow up with crooked teeth, and those who do can still realign them if willing to endure braces for a time (like one member of a famous singing group who appears on television, dental hardware and all). But there's no predicting what it may do to your love life. One older woman upon getting dentures was almost pleased to be rid of the two big front teeth of which she had always been ashamed. When her husband returned from a trip, there she was with nice small front teeth. However, he was griefstricken. Seems he had been fond of those two teeth. They were, he said dejectedly, the only way he could tell her from all the other women.

I once knew a young woman who decided her whole problem with men was her looks. (It wasn't. It never is.) And her special spite was her teeth. I thought they gave her a kind of cute, crooked smile but they definitely didn't look like that to her so she put herself in hock and appeared with a mouthful of hardware that rivaled George Washington's. And lo and behold, right in the middle of braces, rubber bands, and semi-intelligibility, along came Prince Charming, took one good look and fell in love, and, for all I know, they're living happily ever after. So if you didn't have your teeth fixed when you were a kid, and are too cheap to do it now, let somebody nice fall in love with you anyway. And if you still don't like your teeth you can always claim they are a sign of your superior mental status. There's a theory that jaws got smaller when primates got smarter and walked upright; they began to get big bulging brains that didn't leave enough room in the head for other stuff. (On the other hand, my dog has an orthodontist and she's no real intellect.) And if you have bad teeth, be grateful you're not an Eskimo wife with a large family to chew for. Of course, Eskimos didn't have tooth decay until we showed them what to eat to get it.

Your dentist not only keeps you from getting hopeless cavities, builds you extra teeth as needed, does crowd control, shines you up enough to revolt any Malaysian, but may, if you happen to be terribly, terribly unlucky, perform one final service, as Paul Revere, silversmith, nightrider, and dentist did for Dr. Joseph Warren after Bunker Hill. Revere was able to identify the doctor's body by the ivory bridgework he had made for Warren. It must be a distressing experience for your dentist as he views your late bicuspids and soliloquizes, "Alas, poor Yorick. I knew him well."

And I beg of you if you have a very distinctive toothprint, do not even think of becoming a vampire. Culprits have been caught by the toothprints they carelessly left in their victims. A man in Aberdeen, Scotland, was convicted of murder by the bite marks he left in his victim. And if you happen to be doing a burglary job and stop for lunch, don't leave half-eaten sandwiches around. Such toothprints have also been known to convict.

And, now, other sage advice. From the Breviary of Healthe, 1552:

Beware of pulyng out any toth;
for pul out one pul out mo.

and a good English proverb:

If you cannot bite, never show your teeth.

And Benjamin Franklin's infallible remedy for toothache:

Viz.—Wash the root of an aching tooth in Elder vinegar,
and let it dry half an hour in the sun; after which it will ache
no more.

This is true.
And a last safety measure from the Talmud:

If kissed by a Narashite, count your teeth.

Jug Handles
and Other
Great Features

*W*HEN CLARK GABLE and Fred Astaire were first suggested for romantic leads, Hollywood considered the duo impossible because they had (as George IV of England had described his seventeen-year-old ones) "uggley" ears. Of course, the Gable and Astaire ears were not as bad as one of Rudolph Valentino's had been. His was an out-and-out cauliflower, but he also had a friend highly skilled in cosmetic camouflage who worked over the unfortunate appendage until it looked quite fine. She then took Valentino firmly in hand and drilled him in what he must tell the studio makeup and lighting people. And, of course, since he had only one wayward ear, he could do his lovemaking in profile. Gable's and Astaire's might be nothing worse than natural jug handles, but they had two apiece which at first glance made them look more like fugitives from the sixth grade than great figures of romance. Fortunately, somebody took the gamble and the studios got very rich off those four ears and what went between and below them.

We do not know how their mothers regarded their ears, but we do know about Marconi's mother.

When Guglielmo Marconi was born on April 25, 1874, the infant had enormous ears. An old servant disapproved of these prominent features but Guglielmo's mother replied poetically and prophetically, "Ah, but he will be able to hear the still, small voice of the air." This apt maternal rejoinder from any other woman would be cause for skepticism, but from Signora Marconi, née Annie Jameson, the odds are it's true. The daughter of a Dublin distiller, she had begun a promising operatic career at Covent Garden. Since her father had invested his whiskey profits in a castle in which to raise his family, she would have been singularly at home in grand opera, to the dungeon born, one might say. So it was too bad for opera but very good for radio when she eloped with an upper-class Italian widower and in due process produced the aforesaid large-eared infant.

She was, aside from poetic utterances, a remarkable woman with an obvious steadfastness of purpose. She proceeded to teach her little Italians English, bring them up in the Church of England, and transform them into accomplished musicians. Guglielmo played the piano. And Mama Marconi encouraged the child's fascination with electricity. By the age of twelve he had gained sufficient mastery to shatter dinner plates. This accomplishment almost set back the whole future of wireless. Papa Marconi, failing to recognize genius in this event, did some smashing himself, systematically destroying the inventor's experimental equipment before the rest of the house should go the way of the crockery.

However, Mother came to the rescue and abetted the setting up of new equipment in the attic among his grandfather's trays of silkworms. (Silkworm-raising was the rage of the day. Even Evangeline Booth, co-founder of the Salvation Army, had a silkworm for a pet when she was a child.)

P.S. Marconi finally grew up to his ears and, anyway, at historic moments they were concealed from the public by headphones as they listened to the still small voice of the air.

Thomas Edison's ear story is more unfortunate, although it bears a resemblance to the serio-comedy of Him Johnson (or was it Her?), the beagle hoisted by its ears by the president to the president's detriment, at least, if not to that of the pooch. (Even if you believe this to be the proper way of elevating a beagle and the beagle doesn't complain, do not do so if 1) you are a president of the United States, and 2) you are surrounded by reporters. In no time, you will have a pack of enraged animal-loving Americans snapping furiously at your heels.)

At about the age when young Marconi was smashing dinner plates, Thomas Edison had taken to gainful employment, having long since sown his scientific wild oats. He had almost killed a playmate with his hypothesis that a child filled with gas from Seidlitz powders will rise like a balloon, and had blown a companion through a fence by rigging up a boiler to run a woodsaw, which turned a nice profit until it blew up, also setting the barn on fire. (Advice to parents: If your child shows symptoms of scientific genius, give it away.) But now at twelve, young Edison was a businessman selling confectionary on the railroad. One day, as he was trying to board a moving train with arms full of his wares, he was rescued by a conductor who leaned down and hauled him aboard by his ears. He heard a snapping noise in his head and was partially deaf ever after, probably from the breaking of ligaments already damaged by an earlier illness.

Edison once joked that it freed him from boring chatter but this was nonsense. When he was concentrating, he was automatically deaf, dumb, blind, and stupid to everything but the problem in his head. Once he couldn't remember his own name. In school, he'd been a total loss, no doubt because his head was more exciting than the head of his teacher.

But the most famous ears, or rather ear, in history belonged to a sea captain by the name of Jenkins. In the year 1731 he was bringing the brig *Rebecca* home from the West Indies when he was boarded by a Spanish *guardacostas* (apparently undisturbed by any thought of twelve-mile off-shore limits). Not only did they steal and mess up the cargo, but their commander, in an ill-tempered moment, lopped off the English captain's ear. Jenkins, outraged at this assault upon his person and upon the sovereignty of a British ship and a British captain, on arriving in England reported the outrage to the king, in this case George II (the thin, dieting one who loved counting out his money piece by piece). The king wasn't too excited about it, but somebody took it up in the House of Commons, whose members did get stirred up. Of course, it took them six years, but when they did get mad, they got fighting mad and remembered they'd been itching for a war with Spain. So they started one, which is known, naturally, as the War of Jenkins' Ear, and that merged into the general messiness of the War of the Austrian Succession, and it must have all been very gratifying to Captain Jenkins, and a salutary lesson to Spanish marauders.

Nowadays, Jenkins could whip around to his nearest plastic surgeon who, if you should be beset on the Spanish Main with unfortunate consequences to your ears, will grow you a new one. It will be so like the real thing that even your own mother could hardly tell the difference except for one little thing: the new ear frame will be modeled after the gorgeous lobes of a Miami dentist. When the new ear is grown (the process is a mite gruesome but the result is said to be just dandy), it makes the one your mother provided look like a homemade nothing. So rather than spoil a masterpiece, the plastic surgeon may throw in a renovation of the old ear too, thereby making both ears not only unrecognizable to your mother but also a reproach to her innate artistry and creativity.

We are very fortunate that our ears, unless they happen to stick out like those of Gable and Astaire, are well out of our line of vision because ears are *weird*, much worse than noses, which really vary very little from one person to another. Fortunately, you really need a three-way mirror for an unexpurgated view (and, believe me, yours are probably not worth the trouble).

Also, fortunately, your ears are not only protected from your own critical gaze, they attract little attention from others who can keep themselves amused during any dull spots in your verbal intercourse by appraising your nose, eyebrows, and mouth, but your ears will elude them. So unless your ear has recently been cauliflowered by some pugilist, or chewed by an overzealous lover, they're probably hardly worth talking about, and totally unmemorable. (Could you sketch the ears of your father, mother, and three best friends? I couldn't, although I'm reasonably sure they had some.) So if you happen to have unusual ears like Camus, Martha Graham, Lizzie Borden, Pope John, Georges Enesco, or Jonas Salk, nobody in the world will ever notice they're unusual, unless a) you become very famous, and b) somebody has to write about famous flawed ears. But, alas, it works the other way too. If you have ears as handsome as President Eisenhower's, as neat (if slightly pixilated) as Winston Churchill's, as princely as the Duke of Edinburgh's, or even as gorgeous as those of a Florida dentist, probably nobody will ever notice unless you hire a press agent or make a habit of ear-dropping in your conversation.

Of course in the Elizabethan era it was a distinction to have ears at all, the royal temper being what it was, and de-earing being one of the more prevalent and gentler punishments of the day. A certain Dr. Leighten, who seemed to disapprove of his queen, was obviously playing fast and loose with his ears when, in his *Zion's Plea Against the Prelacy*, he called his volatile sovereign "a daughter of Hell, the Episcopacy Satanical." I don't know exactly what the latter phrase means but Elizabeth undoubtedly did and the only surprise is that the erudite cleric escaped with his life, if not with his ears. He was also hastily degraded from his ministry, whipped, branded, pilloried and imprisoned, but all's well that ends well. After a long prison term, he was informed that his punishments had been illegal.

The quaint but understandable custom of de-earing authors was not limited to the Tudors.

The American Colonies did not neglect their writers, particularly the authors of religious heresies, but were more preoccupied with other miscreants. Virginia had a particular aversion to hog thieves, and as late as 1771 in Newport, a counterfeiter named William Carlisle had his ears cropped. Our less-than-charming ancestors may have braved the Atlantic in leaky tubs for the right to worship God in their own way, but God help anybody else with the same idea. Should a Quaker, for example, cross their path, so much the worse for the Quaker—and his ears. The Massachusetts Colonial Records in 1757 lays down the law: "A Quaker if male, for the first offense, shall have one of his ears cut off; for the second offense, have his other ear cut off." And things got worse from there. They were, however, gentler with Quakeresses, who were only severely whipped.

For crimes less heinous than hog-stealing or Quakery, one might merely get pilloried with one's ears tacked to the boards to keep one tidily in place. (The origin of the expression "pinning their ears back," perhaps?)

Except for pirates and penal codes, most people through history have tried to augment the ears rather than diminish them, although it's true President James Buchanan and Herbert Spencer might have enjoyed their hearing more with less effective ears. Buchanan's ears were so acute he could hear things whispered in the next room. His feeling about this would be very puzzling to the White Houses of our time. Rather than profiting by his built-in bugging devices, the president was often embarrassed by their inadvertent invasion of the privacy of others.

Herbert Spencer, the English philosopher, carried a pair of ear plugs to protect his sensibilities if conversation should get too exciting, unlike Samuel Johnson who, when the discourse became not to his liking, "withdrew his thoughts and thought upon Tom Thumb" or Thomas

Edison who could always invent a little something if the conversation got dull or he couldn't hear it.

Even if Edison didn't find loss of hearing a great hardship, most people do, and since the first child put its ear to an animal horn and heard sounds magnified, mankind has tried to improvise hearing aids. Mankind, that is, except Thomas Alva Edison, that arch-inventor with 1,092 patents to his name, who never bothered to invent anything for his own or anybody else's hearing loss, although he got scores of letters from the deaf, and knew the basic principles very well. When he listened to the phonograph, he put his head very close to or against the instrument, believing this enabled him to hear through the inner ear. He also listened to the piano with his head against the instrument.

But if Edison wasn't inventing hearing aids, it seems everybody else was. The results are a tribute both to man's ingenuity and the triumph of imagination over common sense. Many of the devices for amplifying sound—the tuba, the megaphone, the first stethoscope, the telephone mouthpiece, the horn of Edison's own phonograph, and, of course, dozens of ear trumpets—were direct descendants of the humble animal horn, invented by nature for several other purposes but not for magnification of sound.

Some ear trumpets were simple cones with wide mouths like a megaphone. The best vibrations, they said, came from porcelain, but it was exceedingly heavy and fragile, so usually plated silver or japanned tin was used. Marvelous convolutions beyond the fanciest ram's horns were tried but found to have confusing echoes. A Dr. McKeown designed an armchair with enormous ear trumpets sprouting from each side of the back to relieve the user from the effort of holding them. There was a collapsible pocket trumpet, and one in a cane; one shaped like a tobacco pipe (good presumably for the masculine image), and, finally, a neat little trumpet worn behind the ear with a tube leading into the ear itself.

Beethoven was one of history's more illustrious ear trumpet users, and Evelyn Waugh, the British writer of satirical novels, one of its most flamboyant. In the 1920s and '30s, even after discreet little trumpets and even electronic amplification were available, Waugh ostentatiously sported a large-sized ear trumpet for his deafness.

Then came the Audiphone and the Dentiphone. Deaf ladies had observed for a long time that the tip of a fan or a knitting needle held firmly against the teeth sometimes worked quite well. (Like Edison with his head against the piano.) The Audiphone was a small harplike device of thin rubber and silken cords. The top of the piece was held against the upper teeth to make them vibrate to the sound waves picked up by the Audiphone, and amplified. The Dentiphone was a box with an easily vibrating rubber diaphragm to be held between the teeth, with a long silken cord hanging out like a kind of antenna.

All these inventions (except Evelyn Waugh's trumpet) were swept away by the electronic hearing aid, which, legend has it, was first developed, not as an instrument for the deaf, but for use by Scotland Yard. After Watergate, there was, one fancies, a sound of surveillance devices being beaten into hearing aids.

But not only should ears look good and hear good, they should also augur well. And what better guide than the ancient Chinese with their esthetic tastes and their know-how with signs and portents of everything including ears.

For beauty and good news in your fortune cookie, the

ear should be firm, fat, upright, long, roundly curved, close to the head, large, wide in the opening, either red or white, sleek, fleshy at the bottom, and with long hairs in it. It also raises your talent, wealth, and honor if they're stuck on higher than your eyebrows. And rejoice if they happen to be red—they foretell a peaceful life. But if they're whiter than your face, also not to worry—while you may have a few troubles, you'll be a nice guy, generous and faithful, and you'll become famous anyway.

But if you can't quite manage the perfect ear, you may have to choose, for example, among Earth Ears, Chess Ears, or the Hanging Over the Shoulder model. Earth Ears are, of course, flat like the earth. With Earth Ears you get a side dish of too many relatives with your wealth, honor, etc., so maybe best forget them and settle for Chess. Chess Ears are round and well shaped (don't ask me why they are Chess ears; the reason is probably inscrutable), and although you start poor and don't get rich till middle age, at least when you get it, it's yours—no sponging relatives.

If you like more adventure but in a seemly way (they come with honor and dignity), Tiger Ears, small, crooked, and close to the head, are an excellent buy. At all cost avoid Arrowfeather. You'll inherit millions but go bankrupt and have to live hither and thither. Mouse Ears are also to be avoided because they're signs of a stealing and stubborn nature, and Faun Ears are good only if you are planning to die young. They provide a blissful childhood but a dreadful adult life. But if you want the very, very highest honors, Nobel prizes and Orders of the Garter, the only recourse is, unfortunately, the Hanging Over the Shoulder type, but with an earldom or two for consolation, I say, let the ears fall where they may.

Still, you can have your dukedom, and I'll take a pair

of funny-looking, middle-European ears that brought their eighteenth-century owner neither wealth nor long life. They're not easy to describe: "The helix [the outer fold] fell straight down and the area enclosed by the lower half of the ear was peculiarly smooth and flat." But through them, Wolfgang Amadeus Mozart heard the music of the spheres, to the very ⅛th of a tone. Given such ears, it would be greedy to ask for more.

In fact, they'd be a bargain even if they came in a package deal with the Hapsburg Jaw, and the Hapsburg Nose, and the Hapsburg Lip. The Hapsburgs were a line of nobility and royalty that proliferated all over Europe from the twelfth to the twentieth century, contributing lavishly to the general messiness of that continent for eight centuries, and, being arch conservatives, retarding its progress wherever possible. In fact, if you were a Hapsburg and *not* conservative you came to mysterious and distinctly unhappy ends.

The jaw, the mere thought of which makes an orthodontist long to start chipping away at its Class III malocclusion, was extremely inconvenient, in addition to its cosmetic disadvantages. The Hapsburgs were strong patrons of the arts from a judicious mixture of narcissism, royal marriage-making which required large portraits in oil carried from court to court throughout Europe, and a respect for art. They, often, knew a good painter when they saw one, with the result that in any museum dentists and art lovers can study with pleasure the Hapsburg Jaw, also the Nose, also the Lip, in the works of El Greco, Velasquez, and Goya, to name a few.

Chins have always been given psychological attributes, being weak, strong, belligerent, etc., for once, an idea that has at least some validity. When shy or ashamed we do sometimes hold our heads down, thus pulling in our chins. When full of confidence, arrogance, bravado, or determination, the head may come up and the chin jut out. So people read the same meaning into chins whose bone formation suggests these poses. But let's see what history says.

You will recall that the Three Little Pigs in times of interspecies confrontation and crisis and living under the threat of lupine explosion, swore by their chins, the moral seeming to be: Have a firm chin if you can but build your house of bricks anyway in case the chin doesn't work.

Dante Alighieri had a jutting chin and is renowned for sticking to his guns or rather his adoration of the divine Beatrice (whom, by the way, he never really knew) through hell and high water. The moral may be that lifelong adoration comes easier if you don't know the adoree too intimately. Martin Luther had a strong chin which needless to say came in handy, and J. P. Morgan's, along with a number of other formidable features, was his fortune.

So the theory is doing fine until you come to Queen Victoria, whose receding chin was about the only retreat ever shown by this willful, opinionated sovereign. Aeschylus, the great Greek dramatist, had even less chin than Queen Victoria but it is not known whether he pushed people around except emotionally by his plays. He was a strong and forceful warrior in a number of battles and a hero at Marathon.

Maria Mitchell, perhaps America's most distinguished woman scientist, an astronomer of great renown, was a leading fighter for women's rights around the turn of the century. Although in an era much addicted to reading

character through physiognomy, her opponents never noticed she had a weak chin, and if they had taken comfort
therefrom, it would not have been for long. A teacher at
that hotbed of radicalism, Vassar, her strong avant-garde
opinions stood out, including the notion that what students wore was their business and whether they went to
class was also their business. Or rather the business of the
teacher to make knowledge so exciting students would not
be able to stay away. And her classes were all of that.

Hetty Green, the multimillionaire, was a woman
whose career creates some ambivalent feelings in feminists. She was undoubtedly one of the most brilliant financial manipulators Wall Street has seen—a credit to the
brains of her sex. She even had the sagacity to pack a re-
volver to protect her from lawyers. And her chin could
hardly have been more determined. In fact, she looked exactly like a witch, with nose and chin almost meeting.
And, alas, for the feminine cause, she was, aside from her
capitalistic genius, as miserable a specimen of humanity,
male or female, as you could picture. Compared to her,
Scrooge was a living doll. Feminists, in fact, might be
smart to start a rumor that Hetty was really a transvestite,
except that they are far nicer and incomparably better
dressed. She looked like a Bowery derelict moving from
one cheap room to another, dressed in filthy, antiquated
clothes. Her pitifully neglected children were so deprived
that when they inherited her multimillions, they still
found little pleasure in life. The boy was crippled for life,
because Hetty was too miserly to have an injured leg doc-
tored.

Although the physiognomists said that a receding forehead gave one a practical bent, and if combined with a
prominent nose and a long face, a tendency to philan-

thropy, it was also often regarded as a sign of ineffec-
tualness, or effeteness, but inasmuch as Casanova, he of
the receding forehead, was one of history's pushier and
less effete figures, this may not be reliable. A bulging
forehead, like those of Socrates, Beethoven, and Immanuel
Kant, was interpreted by the layman as evidence of bulging intellect (although the brainy part of your brain isn't
up front) and as evidence of childhood rickets by the medical profession, so we'll have to take a detour and hypothesize that the rickets meant the kid was sickly and sat
around the house with nothing to do except read and develop its brains and become a genius.

You can generate a theory to take care of anything. But
some theories are very encouraging, like the one that says
coarse features go with originality of mind. Physiognomy
also provides useful alibis. For example, if you're terrible
at math it's all because your eyebrows turn down at the
ends, so you lack the ability to perform accurate numerical
calculations, like Lord Lyttelton, eminent English historian, who was floored by the multiplication table, doomed
presumably by the ends of his eyebrows.

But such difficult choices: with a short, round neck
you get sagacity (and collars that wrinkle); with a long,
thin neck you get affability. And if you have a wide
mouth in a narrow face you're a whiz at animal imitations,
in case it's a talent you ever need. With a round face you
should have the power of judging the time of year, the
seasons, and the revolutions of the planets, which, I guess,
means that you're in tune with the universe, or you can
rent yourself out to NASA, or, at least, save the price of
an almanac. If you're a little puffy just above the ends of
your mouth you'll be interested to know you've got aqua-
sorbitiveness—a relish for water, drinking, bathing, view-

ing (oceans, lakes, streams, swamps, mud puddles). Lest this seem a pallid attribute, I hasten to add you also like it spiked with alcohol.

If you're going to wrinkle up your face, please do it with forethought. For example, if you have both perpendicular and horizontal lines above the nose, this endows you with the capability of producing propositions in consecutive order. The illustrations omit Euclid but include A Selfish Cat. (Perhaps you have been unaware that when your cat is sitting selfishly in your favorite chair, it is also thinking in beautifully logical concatenations of thoughts.)

But whenever you put the wrinkles, wrinkle. A smooth, round face, no lines, is a terrible giveaway that you are fallaciously subtle and full of sophistry. But only if you are Anglo-Saxon. The Chinese value the calm spirit and unlined countenance. So if you are Caucasian, wrinkle away and don't get your face lifted. A face-lift may ruin your character and capacity for propositions in consecutive order. On the other hand, if you are Oriental, and find you can't avoid wrinkling, pick your lines carefully or you could develop a crawling snake line which is a sign you'll die traveling.

Not only should your lines be etched in with care, you must have just the right moles in just the right places. Depending on where it is, a small mole on your forehead can bring you tremendous wealth, a voice in public affairs, a cruel nature, life in the mountains, or it may prove, happily (unless you happen to be a monk), that you are unsuited to the monastic life.

So, look into your face once more and consider its potential. Think of where you've been together and how long you've had it. You may find you are more attached to it than you thought you were. It is after all yours and, therefore, to you, the world's leading face. Sometimes, I think I'd like my face remodeled a bit here and there for the sake of esthetics but something in me says stubbornly: It's got a right to be the way it is. It's even entitled to grow old. It's lived long enough to have that right. It has merited your loyalty. (On the other hand, suppose somebody shows up with a quick, cheap, painless method for erasing lines? We-l-l, maybe a little under the chin, and a trace here, and a bit over there for good measure.)

And maybe being beautiful isn't so great. My most beautiful patient, so lovely that she would still be beautiful in a burlap bag, cares very little for it. She would rather, she says, be able to sing!

All Hands
and Feet

*T*HE FEET THAT CARRY us—walking, climbing, running toward joy and away from fear—the hands that care for us, dressing, feeding, earning our livelihoods; that comfort, caress, cradle, ward off, strike out; that put together and take apart—these are the servants of the body, performing with equal obedience the most menial and the most exalted of human acts.

While you might think that, in view of their importance, hands and feet should be judged by their competency, this has never been completely true. An amputation or a paralysis is clearly a flaw (unless you are a belligerent type in need of an iron fist), but what about limbs that are considered attractive even though they don't work too well—the tiny, fragile hands of ladies in the Age of Chivalry, for example? How do you figure out what's a flaw? And how much of a flaw?

Consider feet for a moment. Large feet ought to be an asset. The human body, teetering on its two hind legs, could well use bigger feet, especially prolonged at the heel, to give it better balance. But people might find large feet esthetically unpleasing.

And styles change. Men now seem quite happy with girls who wear size 10; only the girls' grandmothers are distressed. Small, dainty hands and feet (such as those of U. S. Grant and John Paul Jones) were once admired even on men. By contrast, George Washington was embarrassed by his large feet.

As for hands, the most efficient arrangement would seem to be hands of different sizes, one for heavy jobs, one for delicate tasks. Men's larger hands are fine for opening jars and changing tires, but men have less fine manual dexterity than women, not because they have poorer coordination but because big fingers get in the way.

If we saw a person on the street with vastly improved hands or feet we would not necessarily be overcome with admiration and envy—quite the contrary. You have often longed for a third hand, so invaluable for tying packages, opening doors when your two hands are full, and for hundreds of other tasks now impossible for us. Yet if we had been born with an extra hand, this wonderful gift would probably have been amputated to save us future embarrassment. There would be no huzzahs for a breakthrough in human development, no interest in breeding a superstrain of humans capable of many new achievements.

Of course many people have had extra fingers. (There's the village of Cervera de Buitnago in the province of Madrid, Spain, where extra fingers are completely normal.) And Francisco Lentini found his extra leg useful for play-

ing soccer, being able to run freely and kick at the same
time.

Toes are not necessarily the most efficient stuffing for
the front of a football boot. They aren't needed inside the
stiff spiked boot and cannot perform their natural function
of grasping and balancing. Something tougher than toes
might be better; at least Ben Agajanian, who doesn't have
toes and who played for the Green Bay Packers, finds it
that way. He can kick the ball to hell and back, or at least
from the yard line. But no doubt the lack of toes embarrassed him when he was a kid and his mother no doubt
shed tears over his poor little baby feet (as a friend of mine
did over her baby's hammer toes, the very same toes for
which she later thanked God because they saved him from
Vietnam).

To most of us a flaw ever so small of hands or feet is a
hardship, a deadly menace, a threat to our very survival.
Arnold Toynbee, that philosopher about history, even
thinks the lame and the weak were earth's first inventors,
driven by the necessity of keeping up with or surviving
against the strong.

When limbs fail we must improvise, so that damaged
feet may walk and weakened arms may work. Undoubtedly the crutch was the first prosthetic device—probably
far older than man. The first little primates to walk
upright full time played with branches, learning, even as
small children today, that sticks are fun for hitting and
hopping, for digging and reaching and hunting. And finally some primate, somewhere, with an injured leg
would discover that he could hobble better leaning on a
stick.

The first crutches we know about belonged to Cinesios, a Greek cither player around 500 B.C., who was so

thin and sickly that he needed limewood supports. Artificial limbs came much later. Fortunately, only civilized people need artificial limbs. Mostly amputations have to await the development of good cutting tools, gunpowder, industrial machinery, and surgeons.

Sharp metal was fortunately available in his hour of need to Hegisistratus, a Greek seer who provided the surgery himself. When imprisoned by the Spartans he cut off his foot, which freed his fettered leg, and he headed for home, thirty miles away at Tigra. As soon as his wound healed he made himself a wooden leg and returned to fighting and soothsaying. The two went together easily, since nobody rushed into battle without first checking which side the gods were on. The seer business also paid well, especially for Hegisistratus (Herodotus hints he was a bit of a money-grubber), whose presence was considered a good omen for any battle. The omens were not, however, too good for the seer himself. The Spartans caught up with him again, and this time put an end to him and his two professions.

Business in artificial legs really boomed after the introduction of gunshot at the Battle of Crécy in 1346 and half-pound gunshot at the Battle of Perugia in 1364 (just as electric wheelchairs have proliferated since the minefields of Vietnam and all kinds of new devices for the handicapped were developed as a consequence of the aerial blasting of Europe in World War II).

Quite naturally, warring knights in need of limbs turned to their armorers for the more personal hardware. Armorers not only had the technical skill required but they also understood a knight's narcissistic needs. And a knight wouldn't be a proper knight unless he looked good, so armorers spent much time on ornamentation. And they carefully matched the designs on prostheses to the knight's baronial armor.

Prince Frederick of Hamburg lost a leg in battle, had a new silver leg made, and, as the chronicle puts it, "continued along his bellicose way." Prince Frederick III of thirteenth-century Germany lost his in a different way. He kicked a door so hard in a fit of pique that he had to have an amputation. There is no record of whether he was careful thereafter to kick something softer, such as a servant.

Peter Stuyvesant damaged his right leg in a military foray in Venezuela. He returned to Holland, acquired an artificial leg, trimmed it with silver (Silver Nails in Connecticut is named for his leg), found himself an attractive and cultivated wife, and set sail for New Amsterdam where, in addition to being a remarkable governor, he was notable for abstaining from drink and swearing a great deal. (New Yorkers have followed his example in the latter if not in the former.)

A surgeon in Rorigo in the 1500s describes an amputee who lost both hands yet could, by means of an iron apparatus, take off his hat, open and close a purse, and sign his name.

Richard III's twisted arm, the one that proved so dramatic in Shakespeare, is puzzling. How a king, surrounded from birth by court gossip, could surprise anyone by displaying it is a mystery. Either the injury was far more trivial than the Bard allows, or the court was the least observant and most circumspect in all royal history.

The court certainly gossiped, and most spitefully, about Anne Boleyn's finger. She was born with big dark eyes (that were to captivate Henry VIII, make her the mother of Elizabeth I of England, and eventually cost her

her head in the Tower of London) and also with a small extra fingernail on one finger. She concealed the fingernail by a fashionable sleeve that came down over her hand in a point, a style that still returns to us from time to time. But her small birth defect was cited as proof positive that she was a witch who had cast a spell on Catherine of Aragon's otherwise devoted husband.

Artificial legs were rarely anything but a handicap in war, but an iron fist was something else again (perhaps the origin of the "iron hand in the velvet glove"?).

A real Captain Hook (possibly the inspiration for the Peter Pan character?) was a Turkish pirate by the name of Horuk Barbarossa who lost his hand in a battle with the Spaniards, after which he wore an iron hand up to the elbow, "very useful in winning battles," as he waged his bloody career. The hook hand is, or is imagined to be, a deadly weapon and appears often in terror movies and TV horror shows.

Gouverneur Morris, who wasn't a ruler but was a descendant of the aristocratic Gouverneur family, was a bon vivant—with or without his pegleg. (He chose a very plain stout piece of oak.) He found time to partake fully of the social whirl of Philadelphia, the gayest of colonial cities, while advising the colonial government on matters of finance. There are several versions of how he came by his pegleg. Probably the dullest—that he sustained multiple fractures after a fall from a carriage—is the true story. But Lord Palmerston's memoirs, more in keeping with Morris's rakish image, have it that he was leaping from a lady's window at the time. Since this was the standard rumor of the day, one can hypothesize that colonial husbands were unusually prone to return at unfavorable times; that colonial windows were most unsuitable for leaping; or that gossips had little originality or creativity. (Even the father of his country was not safe from the cliché. The fatal cold, actually acquired from the old man's stubborn habit of riding in inclement weather, was said to have resulted from his leaping scantily clad from a lady's window.)

A British peer known to us only as Sir Robert R. lost his hand under circumstances he (very wisely) never chose to explain. While with the English army in Scotland, he seduced a local girl who had, it turned out, a very irritable brother. The brother swore vengeance and challenged Sir Robert to deadly combat. Sir Robert refused. The enraged young man thereupon joined Sir Robert's regiment the day before the Battle of Culloden; in the heat of that particularly nasty fray, he ignored both the English and the Scots, zeroed in on his own private foe and hacked off the offensive hand.

Lord Nelson's affair with another man's wife was conducted with neither hasty leapings from windows nor murderous avengers. The admiral was as highly esteemed by the cuckolded husband, Lord Hamilton, as he was by their jointly beloved Emma. When he lost his arm properly and gallantly by cannonball in the Battle of Teneriffe, he ordered the surgeons to make haste. "I know I must lose my right arm, so the sooner it is off the better." Two days later he was busily writing letters with his other hand. But the remainder of his mained arm was restless, a reliable barometer giving him forecasts of a change in the weather ("dampness," he would predict), and, when he was worried or excited, moved back and forth in a paddling motion. "The admiral is working his fin," the sailors said.

But the Nazis paid perhaps the highest compliment an amputee has ever received to a British Royal Air Force pilot by the name of Douglas Bader. Bader had lost both legs in an RAF accident before the war. His artificial legs allowed him to walk and to fly a plane, and when, in World War II, England needed pilots, he returned to the RAF. Half a dozen medals later, he was shot down and captured. The Germans showed their profound respect by incarcerating him in Colditz Castle, a top-security prison for POWs. This was a prisoner they did not want out on the loose, legs or no legs.

Of course many other notable (and ordinary) people have managed extremely well with less than the desirable quota of hands and feet. Sarah Bernhardt, even when forced to remain seated throughout the play, continued to be known as one of the greatest actresses of her generation; Herbert Marshall limped so handsomely that if one noticed his war souvenir at all it added to his distinction; Martyn Green carried on his fine Gilbert and Sullivan portrayals after the disastrous run-in with a Manhattan parking garage elevator that cost him his foot.

And in politics, Senator Inouye of Hawaii, a Democrat of royal lineage (considerably more royal, as a matter of fact, than that of William the Conqueror or Peter the Great), wears an empty sleeve, reminder of brave action in World War II. His missing arm provided one of the most dramatic moments of the Senate Watergate hearings. A lawyer, talking to the press and irked by the senator's searching questions, used a sneering epithet about cripples. The committee, in bipartisan outrage, stopped the proceedings long enough to administer a sharp rebuke to the offender. Senator Inouye himself, long inured to his loss, was obviously far more moved by his colleagues' lusty championship than he had been by the epithet.

You may think it comparatively easy to be a senator or

even an actor with a missing limb, but naturally one cannot be an athlete. Wrong again. Young Ron Suemnick played six games as tackle for his Huron, Michigan, high school football team before he was thrown out of the league for wearing illegal extra equipment—an artificial leg. The Huron school board took the case to court. The judge's decision said in part: "This young man has been an inspiration to everybody, demonstrating what you can achieve against great odds. To deny him the right to play due to the enforcement of a rule of dubious legality would not be in the public interest." Ron Suemnick played his final game of the season under a court injunction. Then, naturally, he went out for basketball.

Pete Gray made it to the major leagues, playing with the St. Louis Browns. He had lost his right arm in a childhood accident but he played all positions on the team, although he did have to redesign his catcher's mitt. In 1945 he played seventy-seven games, batting 218. He was very popular, and the day he smashed a double to win against the Athletics, the fans went wild.

But the all-time star was Three Finger Brown, a pitcher in the 1920s. (Since his real name was Mordecai and since the nickname was used with affection by his fans, and with respect, and sometimes fear, by his opponents, maybe it isn't so bad.) Without his right index finger he was able to cup the ball so that its dipping and weaving drove the opposing team crazy. The Brown Twist made him one of the greatest pitchers of his day.

Pegleg Anglesey (the Marquis of), commander of British forces in Africa, probably didn't mind his soldiers' nickname for him, since the Angleseys had an old family custom of shedding limbs for king and country. A much earlier Marquis lost his at Waterloo. It didn't seem to slow him down much, at least not in pursuit of the ladies. He ran off with the wife of another lord. This story is detailed in the memoirs of Anglesey's friend, that remarkable Regency courtesan Harriette Wilson.

Some amputees prefer to manage without artificial limbs. General Dan Edgar Sickles was known as the Yankee King of Spain for his popularity and influence as United States minister to Madrid. He lost a leg at Gettysburg, had the most up-to-date artificial limb made, stashed it in a closet and for the ensuing forty-nine years used crutches most skillfully and unobtrusively. He married late in life and was blessed not only in his choice of a wife but in his future mother-in-law, who proclaimed that he was very gallant, he had great force, and "wore his crutches as though they were medals—as he should." Not only was he a brave soldier and an accomplished diplomat with excellent taste in wives and mothers-in-law, but he left New Yorkers one of their happiest legacies: in 1852, he secured Central Park for the city.

Central Park as we know it owes its existence to another man on crutches. At the time Frederick Law Olmstead designed the park—so well that it seems not the work of man but a particularly gracious work of nature— he was on crutches, having been thrown from a carriage. Later, this indefatigable man helped found the American Museum of Natural History, the Metropolitan Museum of Art, and the New York State Charities Association. His city has much cause to be glad for his fortitude in the face of adversity.

Many famous people have had club feet or other forms of early crippling. Medical history buffs get particular fun out of arguing about diagnoses of such ancient problems. They still haven't, for example, been able to decide whether the disabled foot of the Pharaoh Siptah was a congenital deformity or the result of poliomyelitis. As for the romantic Lord Byron's foot problem, they can't even agree which foot it was. We can only be certain that he had one crippled foot (or two) as a consequence of a congenital malformation (or maybe polio or cerebral palsy or *something*) that in any case would have darkened his childhood if his mother had not already attended to that; that it made him bitter and the bitterness gave him a dark aura utterly irresistible to women. The foot or feet (as the case may be) rarely seem to have interfered with anything he really wanted to do, whether in literature, sex, or derring-do.

A young Regency rake by the name of Barry seems not to have been put off in the least by his club foot. His place in history hinges on a single event. One night, in an excess of high spirits, he rode his horse up the grand staircase of Mrs. Fitzhebert, mistress of the Prince Regent, and, despite his and his companions' superb horsemanship, none of them knew how to get a horse *down* a staircase. Two burly workmen had to be called in to apply the psychology and brute force necessary to evict the unwelcome house guest.

Thaddeus Stevens was one of the most brilliant speakers, warped minds, and hated men who ever passed through the United States Congress. His bitter hatefulness was attributed by others and apparently by himself to the fact of having been born with a club foot, although it should be noted that a good many men have achieved hatefulness without a club foot. (It may be that he was destined to be obnoxious anyway.)

Their childhood polios left few marks on the psyches of Sir Walter Scott and Chief Justice William O. Douglas, except perhaps to make them more physically and mentally adventurous. Young Scott, with his lame foot, was so avid a forest tramper that his father complained "he must have been born to be a strolling peddler," an idea the boy found quite inviting. Unlike Sir Walter, who had a lame leg all his life, Justice Douglas came out of his bout with nothing much worse than legs that were rather weak and spindly for a time. At the suggestion of a playmate, he began to climb mountains for exercise, forming an addiction that he could never shake. (Hiking boots were the most important item in his young wife's trousseau.)

So many people have had crippled feet, that a mere limp, like those of the composers Handel and Gounod, the great chemist Sir Humphrey Davies, Elias Howe, inventor of the sewing machine, and Queen Alexandra of the Edwardian era, are hardly worth mentioning.

Lafayette was badly wounded twenty yards from the British lines at Brandywine, but in the excitement of the moment didn't notice. Ironically, he recovered very well from his battle wounds only to come to grief from a simple fall in Paris, when he broke the neck of his left thigh bone. Being a radical, he tried the newest, most radical procedure for such injuries. His treatment called for forty days of stretching on a rack, to which he submitted without complaint. Unfortunately, a strap of the apparatus cut into the thigh and gangrene set in. It was arrested, but left his knee and hip permanently stiff from the treatment.

The history of modern warfare almost took a different turn with the twisted knee of a West Point cadet. The football injury, added to his assortment of other problems at school, almost tempted young Dwight Eisenhower to give up the battle. The accident, just before the Army-Navy game in 1912, ended his sports career, except for coaching. He had also boxed and wanted to be a baseball player. He became so despondent that, on several occasions, he almost resigned from West Point.

But he was neither so despondent nor so incapacitated that he and his girl friend (pre-Mamie) could not shock the chaperones at a party by the abandon of their dancing. Ike, who was often in disciplinary hot water, was broken from sergeant to private for this offence. Since by the time penalties were meted out he was on crutches, and one of his punishments was doing tours of the grounds, discouragement seems reasonable.

Lincoln once said that the only requirement for the length of a man's legs was that they be long enough to reach the ground. Zachary Taylor would also have liked his long enough to get on a horse easily, but they weren't. He had to have an orderly assist him.

John Quincy Adams was not quite as uncomplaining as Lafayette and Eisenhower. It irked him that he could not use his right hand well and he said it slowed down his writing. At the age of two, he had been snatched out of the path of a carriage with such force that his right shoulder was damaged for life (probably dislocated). The nerve plexus was injured and his arm never grew properly nor attained normal strength.

President Andrew Johnson, while in Congress, broke his wrist in a riding accident. It was set badly and made writing so painful that his speeches were handwritten by somebody else although the words are his own. But the most execrable handwriting of any president belonged to Martin Van Buren, for whom there seems to have been no excuse, although some people speculate kindly that he may have been forced as a child to change from right- to lefthandedness.

Abraham Lincoln's trouble was feet. He had corns on

his toes, and at every opportunity would take off his shoes while Mrs. Lincoln hurriedly ordered slippers to cover the large gauche spectacle.

The first Duke of Bedford in the seventeenth century had kept a neat accounting of the cost of his corns: half a crown to five shillings for his chiropodist. He could, of course, have gotten the service cheaper from one of the street-vendors who hawked their services, "Corns to pick. Corns to pick."

Robert Schumann, like many pianists, did not like his fourth finger. The fourth is the weakling, and slower than its brethren. But Schumann set out to do something about his. He fitted out an exercise apparatus with springs and counterweights and sentenced the offending digit to long hours of vigorous exercise from which it never recovered and gave him trouble for the rest of his life.

Ravel composed his famous *Concerto for the Left Hand* for a Viennese concert pianist, Victor Wittgenstein, who had lost his right arm in World War I. Wittgenstein made a successful world tour with it.

That the super-normal should sometimes be demanded of hands and feet—juggling, tight-rope walking, weight-lifting, tap dancing—is understandable, but what about people who deliberately give up even the normal functioning of hands or feet? There are African and Asian tribes that require the sacrifice of a finger as a mark of membership or a measure of bravery. Or the Mandarin Chinese who for centuries deformed the feet of half their children, because abnormally tiny feet made a woman more beautiful and more marriageable (lotus blossom feet they called them). They bound the feet of little girls to arrest normal growth, subjecting the children to much pain and, sometimes, even to death from gangrene.

While Western children escaped this torture, Western

women often inflicted it upon themselves with shoes too small or too pointed. When everything else was covered by voluminous skirts, feet were a strong focus of sexual attraction. A tiny foot and a stolen glimpse of a trim ankle could be very on-turning to our grandfathers or great-grandfathers (who seem to have been a sexier and more excitable lot than their descendants).

While women's feet were a stellar attraction, legs were hardly important at all, since they were never seen except in music halls, or in boudoirs where other anatomical lures took precedence. But a *man's* leg was something else again. When men wore skintight breeches, a trim calf was vital to a man's allure.

But all this is trivia compared to the dilemma of Arthur Macmurrough Kavanaugh. On the morning of March 25, 1831, when the doctor broke the monstrous news to an Irish member of the British Parliament that his third son had been born with neither hands nor feet, Captain Kavanaugh and his heartbroken young wife could only pray that the child would not survive the day. Their prayer went unanswered, perhaps because it could not be heard above the lusty lungs of a stouthearted infant announcing that he had arrived and had every intention of remaining.

Within a few months, the doomed, unwelcome infant had transformed himself into a much-loved, laughing cradle-dweller soon to be a delightful small child carried around on willing shoulders or, seated in a special little basket seat, led about on his fat pony. He grew into a lively, fair-haired, singularly engaging boy, writing his lessons in a small graceful script by means of a hook attached to his shoulder. (This device would eventually enable him to draw, fish, sail, ride to hounds, and drive a four-in-hand of ponies at breakneck speed.) He would live most of his life on horseback when not at home, sailing, or driving. He seemed quite naturally to be the leader among his cousins and other young fry because of his capacity to foment the best adventures and the most ridiculous pranks.

Since his disability made Eton or Harrow impractical, his now widowed mother decided to substitute travel, in whose educational properties she had great faith. She first took Arthur to France and Italy to learn the languages and as an aperitif before undertaking the arduousness of serious Victorian travel.

Their agenda called for an expedition to Egypt, a few months of life on a Nile houseboat, then a pilgrimage across the Sinai Desert in the path of Moses and the ancient Israelites, and a visit to Jerusalem, returning home at the end of two years by way of Italy. The party was comprised of Arthur and his older brother, Tom, with their essential arrays of sporting guns and old shooting jackets; Lady Kavanaugh, with easels and painting paraphernalia; a younger sister, with boxes and jars for collecting specimens; a tutor-clergyman and his clerical riding breeches and boxes of classics to be introduced into his pupils' heads as they traversed mountain and desert; and, of course, a suitable supply of Bibles, prayer books, and English medications.

Young Arthur had a marvelous time, combining, in the manner of Victorian gentlemen, a reverence for biblical history with a passion for destroying as many as possible of God's creatures. "The best shooting in the world," wrote Arthur in his mandatory, Victorian journal, "is on the Nile, with wolf and wild boar and hyena hunting and coursing gazelles with beautiful Persian greyhounds." His brother added in his journal, "His [Arthur's] shooting is as wonderful as his riding. He has shot a great many geese and snipe." And they used hounds again to hunt wolves outside Jerusalem. Arthur found a kinship with the Bedouins and their horses, and although the youngest in the party, he learned Arabic quickly and served as guide and spokesman. The Bedouins, like everybody else after the initial shock, thought little of his infirmities and much of his personality and horsemanship. And he made a fine appearance in his frieze hunting jacket with a black kilt thrown casually across his limbs as he sat on his spirited Arabian steed, handsome, broad-shouldered, always well groomed.

The Sinai was exciting. "We enjoyed the desert immensely. In fact, we had a very jolly time of it. At Hebron, we exchanged camels for the Syrian horse." Arthur described his horse lovingly: ". . . his coat shining like glass; his eye and the expression of his countenance, *fiery* yet *sweet*." The only painful part of the journey was parting. "Poor beast! I cried the day I left him. He knew me so well! He used to lick my face when I came out of the tent in the morning to see him."

But Arthur and animals always had a special affinity for one another. Once he came riding home with an ape bought from a sailor at the harbor, the ape sitting beside him like a gentleman of breeding, a pose it lost when without Arthur's influence; it dashed up the staircase and snatched a pearl necklace from the neck of a surprised lady who happened to be descending. It then ate the pearls with relish. In Arthur's middle life, a small, tame bear followed him or sat decorously beside him as he conferred with tenants and neighbors.

The traveling party returned from the Holy Land to an Irish rebellion (the one of 1848), and Lady Harriet feared Tom, and even young Arthur, might become embroiled. Her fears were fully justified. Arthur went out one night to reconnoiter a rebel camp and was saved from capture only because he was an experienced cross-country rider. His mother was not amused. "There is to be no more of this kind of thing," she proclaimed and shipped Arthur, his brother, and their long-suffering tutor-cum-spiritual-mentor off on another expedition, this time far more daring—through Finland, Russia, Kourdistan, Persia, and, finally, India; a remarkable itinerary for any mother to approve, since the first two Englishmen to risk the projected route through Kourdistan had been most foully murdered. Lady Kavanaugh could never be regarded as the overprotective mother of a severely crippled child, but I suspect the family had long since forgotten that Arthur was more vulnerable to danger than his brother. And as it turned out, he wasn't.

Arthur Kavanaugh proved to be one of life's survivors, and this time he, except for a manservant (sent home early because of illness), was the only survivor.

Tragedy did not strike until India. Meanwhile, Arthur's journal told of wild adventure: of crossing turbulent rivers on rafts of goatskin, of sleeping in holes dug in the snow, of racing through burning tree tops to escape a prairie fire, of clinging to mountain passes so treacherous that the pack donkey just ahead of him stumbled and fell into the abyss. They hunted gazelles with the glorious Kourd Khan who proved, according to Arthur, to be an atrocious bore. In order to keep hunting, Arthur had been keeping a fever down with quinine. Soon after he arrived in Persia, the illness finally became acute. His hunting companion, a young Persian prince, took Arthur home to be nursed back to health in the harem by an old woman who had been informed by the prince that Arthur was a god. During his convalescence, she used to conduct him to the ladies' quarters for a change, an experience that he described not as romantic or exotic, but heart-rending. The ladies told the sympathetic young man their stories of being torn away from their homes, never again to see their loved ones.

Despite the company of these amiable ladies and the lavish hospitality of the prince, Arthur was glad to leave their ancient splendor. "Their compliments and their never-ending lies are enough to disgust any man with common sense," he wrote in British disdain (and ingratitude?).

Although they all arrived in India more or less sick, they found the country enchanting with its gorgeous spectacles and its tiger shoots. (They killed two.) But there Arthur's journal ends. His older brother became desperately ill. Only a long sea voyage, the physicians said, could cure him. He and the tutor must take all available money and sail at once for Australia, leaving Arthur behind in India. Tom did not live to complete the voyage. Their faithful teacher-companion, whose duties had taken him over routes and through dangers seldom faced by scholars, was killed in an accident in Australia. For the first time in his life, Arthur was confronted by the full weight of his physical limitations. He was totally alone and penniless; money did not arrive from Ireland for six long months. He often had only one meal a day. It hurt his pride to be forced to ask for assistance. The news of his brother's death was overwhelming. His infirmities seemed unbearable and his circumstances intolerable.

So he got a job. He became a dispatch rider, making

fast, arduous cross-country rides from post to post in all kinds of weather, and managed to eke out a living. After a time, he found a better appointment, in the surveying department of the East India Company at the phenomenal beginning salary of £400 a year. By this time Arthur Kavanaugh was twenty.

A promising East India career seemed ahead of him but his only surviving brother died and Arthur inherited Borris, the family estate, which he must now settle down to manage. He had less and less time for sport, except an occasional day of fishing, a trip to Norway, or a short cruise on his schooner to the Ionian Isles. While in India, he had settled the issue of marriage in his twenty-one-year-old mind. He reasoned that he had taken many risks in life and had known when he could trust himself, and concluded that he could make a wife happy. His opinion proved justified, but the scales may have been tipped slightly by the fact that he was much in love with a distant cousin, who, it transpired, had also been pining for him.

When he came into his estate, they married and produced seven perfectly normal, happy children who filled the house with games and laughter; yet it was their father who gave the home its special quality with his kindness, his hospitality, and his high spirits, as ready for ridiculous pranks as he had been as a child.

Kavanaugh said of himself that he was proud, inconsistent, and that he *terribly* wanted things it was impossible for him to have. I'm sure this was achingly true but it is difficult to see where in an already overflowing life he could have crowded them in. He was the kind of man who saw more adventurous possibilities and more work to be done than can be encompassed in a lifetime by any number of hands and feet. A sketch of his typical day is enough to give the physically unimpaired reader a feeling of exhaustion.

He became an extraordinarily competent landlord, so highly respected that even the Fenian Raiders left his village and estate unmolested. His judgment was sought by tenants with their family problems, and he was often asked to sit on public commissions. He first became high sheriff of Kilkenny, then lord lieutenant, and was finally persuaded to stand for the British Parliament, did so and was elected. No one seemed to think his infirmities a handicap for public office (or fierce political controversy) any more than his mother had perceived them as a barrier to hazardous travel.

The inscription on his tomb in the little ruined church on Bally Coppigan at Borris reads: "Well done, thou good and faithful servant," a tribute surely merited but tame for a life so versatile and adventurous.

Noses of
Distinction

*I*F YOU HAVE looked your nose in the face for the thirty-thousandth time and concluded that it is not now nor has it ever been the nose of your choice, then by all means buy a new, beautifully expurgated version. But before you rush off to your nearest plastic surgeon there are important decisions to be made. No riffling through his catalogues and ordering any old, or rather new, nose that hits your fancy. Your whole future may depend upon your nose. No impulse-buying. Fortunately, you will have time for this while you negotiate the sale of your dear old grandmother or perform what other legerdemain is required to raise the price. You will also have time to long for the days of Merrie and Cheap Olde England when you could do your own nose job with Alex Ross's Nose Machine which "applied to the Nose for one hour daily so directs the soft cartilage of which the member consists,

that an ill formed Nose is quickly shaped to perfection."
And all for ten shillings and sixpence, or, if you wished to
be very sub nosa about your nasal transfiguration, for an
extra tuppence you could have "secret packaging." Or if
they still have a caste of Khangars in India, as they had in
ancient days, who can "reshape a nose, however it's
wanted," you may wish to comparison-shop. Perhaps you
can get your rhinoplasty and a round trip by Air India for
the cost of a California Special. Remember those East Indians and their beautiful noses (with or without jewels?).
Do you think there may be something they haven't been
telling us?

But in any case, before you precipitate yourself heed-
lessly into a new nose you must consider the fashion trend
in noses. Will your nose be passé in a few years (perhaps
even before you've made your final payment) and have to
be traded in? Now, eighteenth-century England liked a
noble nose for a noble face, and nobles like Lord
Brougham who possessed this large aristocratic trademark
often chose to have it recorded for history in profile paintings or even in paper silhouettes, which were all the rage
at the end of the eighteenth century, although it must be
said that George IV seemed very pleased with his *petit nez
retroussé*. He was a patron of the arts and very susceptible
to foreign tastes (like his famous Chinese Pavilion at Bath),
so perhaps there was a French influence in his attitude
toward his un-English nose. France has always admired
the retroussé and often attributed magical and dangerous
powers to its uplift, especially if found on the female face.
"A little retroussé nose," one writer declared, "may over-
throw the laws and the government." But futures in the
retroussé nose are hard to define, since it is difficult to say
whether the popularity of overthrowing laws and nations

is waxing or waning (but what investment is certain these days?).

The great Hollywood empire demanded the Grecian profile. The color tube epoch inclines toward the all-American hit-or-miss he-man appendage. Despite the difficulty in predicting trends (even *Women's Wear Daily* seems not to have taken a position on this issue), the possession of a fashionable nose has never been so crucial. Time was when you could be remembered for your à la mode nose no matter what you really possessed, painters and sculptors having no wish to have their work marred by unseemly and outdated noses. (Rudolph of Hapsburg had so large a nose that no artist would ever paint its full dimension.) If you harbor a suspicion that the classical Greek noses on those classical Greek statues probably first saw the light of day on the statues and not on the models, you're probably right. For if you yourself had ancestors and have not had to sell their portraits to support their descendants, you have observed that their noses came and went with the tides of portrait fashion. Now in the age of television and the talk shows and camera vérité, only your plastic surgeon can keep the world from knowing the *worst*.

But more important than fashion will be the risk you run to your personality and future by altering your nose. Physiognomists tell us our faces are our fortunes, the harbingers of our destinies. The nose, they proclaim, tells what we will be. From the ancient Chinese to the ardent Victorians (that's why their letters were crammed with physical descriptions), no snipping or molding would possibly be permitted without the guidance of a nasal oracle. Suppose, for example, your plastic surgeon, not being either Chinese or Victorian, innocently snips years off your life—a long nose and a long life having gone hand in glove since antiquity. Or, what if you find yourself with the nose of a lecher, murderer and congenital idiot (in the book, it's a perfectly good-looking nose). Even if you do not thereafter actually lech, murder, or lose your marbles, how do you know your next job interviewer or prospective love object will not be versed in the ancient lore of physiognomy, and being unable to recognize the basic you behind the nose job, reject you posthaste under the mistaken impression that you are a murderer and a congenital idiot. (Lechery is, of course, okay since sex became a joy.)

So you must bone up carefully on the portent of your present and future noses, for surgeons, I hear, are chipping away at creativity and snipping off moral courage in the most feckless, if lucrative, fashion. Let me give you a few illustrations of what you will be, according to the Chinese, ipso facto gaining or losing with your new nose.

A straight, fat nose is a sign of a long life. (But beware the short, flat, or crooked one. It's a sign of bankruptcy, or maybe a sign you're stupid, and in either case you'll get no help from your wife's brother.)

If your nose and the central section of your face is too long, be glad if you live in a democracy because you'll have no chance of winning the king's favor. We can, however, highly recommend the Dragon Nose (full, straight tip, straight high bridge); Tiger Nose (small at each side of tip, inconspicuous nostrils, high bridge); or Rhinoceros Nose (projects straight from the forehead). They all signify wealth, honor, and fame or, at least, high government position where no doubt one could then, as now, also find ways to augment one's capital.

With the Lion Nose, the wealth will unfortunately come and go. The investment firm that chose a lion as its talisman and trademark had perhaps failed to consult the wisdom of the ancient Chinese. With a Garlic Nose (shape only) you don't get prosperous till middle or old age and it makes your brothers unhappy. A Dog Nose makes you loyal but prone to steal when poor. With an Ape Nose you have a fondness for fruit and flowers but a hot temper. The Chinese either have more appreciation of animal noses as works of art than we do, or they don't care how a nose looks so long as it means well. But one must study their lore carefully, not only so you can avoid Lion Noses if you're going heavily into the stock market but to escape worse fates. Suppose your plastic surgeon leaves you suited for nothing but the monastic life! Having given it much thought, I myself have selected the Orangutan (high-bridged, symbolizing a liberal and broad mind, and a heroic and virtuous nature), with a bit of Mongol Goat (to supply the great honor and wealth), although on further reflection that's essentially what I'm now wearing. Hooray, I can save the price of rhinoplasty and just sit around waiting for the wealth, honor, and heroic nature to emerge.

In addition to a sound background in physiognomy, you must foresee the lifestyle into which you wish to fit the new nose and select one suitable to these ambitions. Suppose you are not now a multimillionaire and wish to join their ranks. You will pore over noses built for the sweet smell of money: the John Paul Getty; the Rockefeller, Nelson (if you like your multimillions with a side dish of politics), or the Rockefeller, David (if you prefer to keep in more intimate contact with your wealth); the H. L. Hunt (do not become confused here and order the E. Howard Hunt by mistake); the Aga Khan (but sneak on an extra quarter of an ounce of nose if you can, since the

Aga Khan is paid his weight in gold by his followers); or the Queen Elizabeth II (not at all a bad nose, and the richest female specimen in the world).

Or perhaps the Nose for News is for you, say the New York Times Seemly of Clifton Daniel (it could never possibly print an unfit thing) or the New York Times Inquisitive of Harrison Salisbury (the quintessence of physiognomy-approved news sniffer-outer, and the sharpest in the field, anatomically and reportorially). On the other hand, this fine bird-dog type nose can lead you into the damnedest places, like a Siege of Leningrad, or Hanoi at times when the United States government would be happy to add both you and *The New York Times* to its bombing missions. So maybe you're better off with the stay-at-home William Buckley Sniffy, except so much of the news you'll receive will be offensive to this sensitive olfactory receptor. The TV Anchorman Nose also stays safely out of dangers except the Wars of the Network Succession, but is particularly susceptible to the vagaries of fashion, thereby probably requiring nose reorientations at regular intervals to escape repatriation to the boondocks. At the moment, the rough and ready, the knobbly, and the cutesy poo seem to be in ascendance, television-wise, and are fast usurping the territory of the Walter Cronkite pontifical, the Howard K. Smith handsome-authoritative and the John Chancellor rectitude personified. David Brinkley, who arrived years ago by sheer merit and without the slightest assist from his then unfashionable nose, now finds himself in the forefront of picture tube trendiness.

If you call the studio in search of photographs on which to remodel your future news-announcing nose, CBS will send you a group array as uninspiring as your last sales convention. Even the photographer had obviously been discouraged by such unnewsworthy features and not given it his finest work. NBC proves even vaguer, as if surprised that anyone could be interested in such a display.

So very different from the pride with which public television displays its prize news purveyors. Large individual glossies suitable for pinups or printing, every nose obviously selected for the place it is to fill in the grand design, once again demonstrating the superiority of PBS over crass commercial television. Not even *The New York Times* has a nose so suited to the gathering and dissemination of news as Big Bird's. Where at CBS is the nose so amenable to cheery and unrepentant weather forecasting as Ernie's? Who at NBC has so good a face for the nightly doom and gloom as Oscar the Grouch, and what better job training than life in a trash can? Just picture it, Henry Kissinger reported by a real pro, like Oscar. The spine tingles at the thought. And what food reporter has the Cookie Monster's total dedication to his assignment and eager grasp of his subject?

Clearly the Major League studios should be attempting to lure these crack players with profitable contracts and inviting trades: say, one "Sesame Street" pro for two ABC White House correspondents.

If you wish, on the other hand, to become president, you can show your plastic surgeon a copy of Washington crossing the Delaware, the nose of which shows its owner to have a high moral character (no bridge), fertility of mind, and little vanity, and whose stance indicates that along with the nose you may be acquiring very little common sense about boats (the smallest child knows enough to sit down). So perhaps you'd better put the presidential yacht in mothballs. If you now happen to have a G.W.

nose you may already have felt that you'd rather have a nose job than country-wide fatherhood. But, of course, you could have the John Adams Pointy, the Andrew Jackson Rough and Ready (the ancient Chinese would have called it a zigzag nose and thought poorly of it), the Lincoln Hawk Nose (supposed to be good for horse-trading), the Wilson Scholarly, the Truman Homespun Sharp, the Texas Expansive, The Nixon Skijump, or the Ford All-American.

In fact, if you want to be president, you can be sure your nose is of presidential quality just as it is—whatever it is.

If you are a woman married to a Sikh, do not be unfaithful, or deny him his conjugal rights. He may revert to ancestral law and bite off your nose. While this would seem to be biting off your nose to spite his eyes, he has the consolation that you won't look too good to your lover either. Unless, of course, the lover happens to be Genghis Khan. The Tartars proclaimed, "The lesser the nose, the greater the beauty," and Mrs. Genghis Khan was the greatest beauty of them all, having scarcely any nose at all except for two openings through which she breathed.

Early travelers in America reported the same husbandly nose-biting-off among the Natchez, Iroquois, and Huron Indians, but you're smart not to take their word for it. The only thing early European visitors had a lower opinion of than white colonials was red natives, except for those romantic travelers who were into noble savages and unspoiled children of nature. And even they seemed grateful to scurry back across the Atlantic, scalp intact.

Rameses II, pharaoh of Egypt, cut off the nose of any subject who talked against him. Another Egyptian ruler, Actisanes, sent prisoners to a distant part of the empire called Rhinoconun (which, since he first cut off their noses, means Noses Cut Off, or Desert of the Noseless, or Noses' Place—my Greek scholar hasn't yet made up his mind).

The nose of the historian Lord Macaulay was sufficiently patrician that he could afford to look down it at celebrities less classically endowed. In recording the Bishop of Ely's escape to the Continent from a charge of treason, Macaulay snidely expressed surprise that the bishop could have traveled unnoticed "for his nose was such as none who had seen it could ever forget."

The Duke of Anjou, a rejected suitor of Queen Elizabeth, and a Frenchman, therefore, ipso facto a double-dealing scoundrel, had a king-size nose. A Dr. Cooke-Taylor rhymed:

> Good people of Flanders pray do not suppose
> It is monstrous this Frenchman should double his nose,
> Dame nature her favors but merely misplaces,
> She had given two noses to match his two faces.

Why noses rate so much attention and angst (nose jobs are the plastic surgeon's bread and butter), who can say. A nose is, after all, except for the ears (unless you happen to be an accomplished ear wiggler from fifth-grade boredom), the most phlegmatic of all your features. The nose rarely bothers to participate in what is going on around it, although capable of crinkling, wiggling, twitching, sniffing, snorting, and flaring. Perhaps because it is immobile while all the other features are active and change appearance constantly, it presents a more fixed image and you can get a bead on it. Maybe it gets attention because it's dead center, or because it sticks out like the prow of a ship. Freud would tell you it's because it's a phallic symbol (a displace-

ment upward is the delicate way Freudians put it), and
sure enough some people, men, women, and children,
with anxieties about that genital detail draw some very X-
ratable noses when asked to make a picture of a person.

Noses are more often the subject of ridicule and attack
than any other part of the face, which according to your
viewpoint seems most unfair since the nose rarely gets involved in emotional displays, or, it's the fitting retribu-
tion for those who refuse to become involved in the problems around them. Noses, of course, are regarded as not
quite proper, because of their sneezy and runny propensities, but this again is most unfair. A cold in the nose is not
in or caused by the nose at all. The nose is purely a good
Samaritan, taking care of trouble caused by those cranial
blackguards, the sinuses. The poets neglect the nose,
while lavishing attention on marble brows, ruby lips, soul-
ful eyes, and hair like a tortured midnight. Although
Shakespeare mentions noses eighty times, in most of the
eighty the owner would have preferred he didn't. When
the Romans said you had nothing but a nose, that meant
you had no particular ability (and *that* was a Roman nose;
imagine if they'd been talking about an Anglo-Saxon
one!).

Noses are regular victims of dreadful puns like this old
English rhyme:

> Although a man's as wise as Solon
> There's more in noses than he knows on.

Perhaps to redress its many injustices, London once had a
nose club, whose members' ranks depended on the length
of their noses; the chairman had the longest, and the crou-
pier had no nose at all.

Now for the classification of noses, a pastime which

has been going on since antiquity. A Florentine museum has an old cameo on which is engraved: "The noses of mankind are divided into six clearly marked and well defined classes." These are:

The Grecian, or Straight
The Roman, or Aquiline
The Cogitative, or Wide Nostriled
The Hawk
The Celestial, or Turned Up
The Snub

The most esthetically prized nose has always been the beautifully chiseled lines of the Greek nose. It must be perfectly straight. "Any undulation would disqualify a nose." The only problem with the Grecian nose is that you've seen it so many times on classical statues and canvases that when you see a real live one, it makes its owner look like an inanimate object. It's hard to picture a Greek nose in lively settings except perhaps some wingding of the gods. It would be impossible at a backyard barbecue or fixing a furnace. They do show up on an upper-echelon face at office parties (and the party dies the moment the Hellenic nose appears). They are, indeed, valued in executive circles and are probably worth an extra ten or twenty thousand dollars.

Naturally, it presages only the highest-class psyche and talent, and is particularly rife among lovers of arts and letters, like Petrarch, Milton, Boccaccio, Raphael, Rubens, Titian, Holbein, Cellini, Voltaire, Byron, and Shelley.

The Roman nose, called by Plato "the Royal nose," is a larger-than-life Greek nose with a hump to it. There are those who have seen Roman history as a cavalcade of the deeds of Roman noses, whose owners naturally possess firmness, strength of will, activity of mind and body, all very good for getting your own way and getting on in the world. For example,

> Julius Caesar and a whole bunch of other old Romans
> King Canute, who, however, at least once failed to get his own way
> William the Conqueror
> Queen Elizabeth I
> Sir Francis Drake
> Christopher Columbus, a determined man
> Stout Cortez
> George Washington
> Duke of Wellington

If you've got a Greek nose, don't pick any fights with Roman noses. You'll get clobbered. As somebody has written, "A Greek Nose (Napoleon's) met a pure Roman nose (Wellington's) at Waterloo, and we know the result." Napoleon himself selected his officers by their noses, believing a stout, strong nose the mark of a strong warrior.

The Greco-Roman merger makes a nice all-purpose nose, especially greatnesswise. There's:

> Emperor Constantine
> Lorenzo de' Medici
> Sir Walter Raleigh
> Leonardo da Vinci
> Christopher Wren
> Purcell

and practically all the Greats:

> Alexander the Great
> Alfred the Great
> Frederick the Great

The Hawk nose is more specialized. This used to be called the Jewish nose but cannot now be so described out of consideration for the Arabs, who distinctly do not wish to have Jewish noses although it's as plain as anything else on their faces that they do, while, according to one past writer, the Jews don't have Jewish noses anymore because it is not an ethnic nose but an occupational nose and the nose of the intellectual Jew of the present day has lost much of the sharpness derived from Syrian ancestors. (Is it tactful to mention ancestors on that side of the family?) Actually the hawk nose seems no respector of race, color, or creed, cropping up on such ethnically diverse faces (none of them traders) as:

Vespasian, a good, progressive Roman emperor
Correggio, a right-talented Italian painter
Adam Smith, a Scots Presbyterian
Felix Mendelssohn, a Protestant composer of Jewish descent
Johannes Brahms

The most hawklike nose of all is the one pictured on the face of Mahomet, in a portrait so overwhelmingly romantic with its dark magnetic eyes that it seems to be the dream of an English Victorian lady in an era when they pined for Sheiks of Araby. (One or two actually got their sheiks. Their daughters merely went to the movies of Rudolph Valentino.) It's always refreshing to find a divinity with sex appeal. So many of them are holier-than-thou. Ah, if the Middle East oil barons only looked like Mahomet, it wouldn't be so bad being bought up by them.

Now we come, alas, to the snub nose, which has had some great owners but a very bad press, at least among European face-readers. The Orientals probably see it differently, and Genghis Khan's physiognomists would, if they valued their skins, see it as divinely beautiful and ordained to bring its possessor great triumphs and joy. But the West gave it short shrift. "The Snub may be best described by enumerating the excellencies of form which it lacks but as I have described," says one author washing his hands of the Snub, "the characteristics to be found in the other classes, I will allow the Snub to speak for itself and we may feel assured that what it says to us will be very plain."

It was explained that while all babies are born with snub noses (presumably, even Julius Caesar), as the mind opens to the world it stretches the nose; ergo, if your nose does not rise and lengthen itself, it indicates the retention of babyish weaknesses. In any case, a snub nose was very troublesome—and expensive—to the family of Tristram Shandy.

His grandfather courted a lady who was a Tartar but unfortunately not a real Tarter. If she had been, the problem would not have arisen, because she would then, like Genghis Khan, have been delighted by the snubness of his nose, but *autres temps, autre mores.* She was so humiliated at the thought of being married to this ignoble feature that she demanded a settlement of £200 a year extra to ease her bruised pride. Even after her husband's nose was dead and buried, the memory of so truncated a member continued to require compensation from his heirs. Surveying this unfortunate depletion of the family coffers, Shandy concluded that "No family, however high, could stand a succession of short noses."

Physiognomists at the turn of the century offered Nero and Caligula as evidence of the dire consequences of arrested development. They did not foresee Winston Churchill's snub nose. Churchill, when offered the opinion that his new grandson (the current Winston Churchill) looked exactly like him, replied, "All babies look like me."

But the deriders of the snub nose get their comeuppance. Whether a Greek nose was Napoleon's Waterloo, a particular snub nose is the downfall of physiognomy and one from which its advocates run like rabbits. For there in the middle of all those straight, beautifully chiseled, artistic Athenian noses, sat the greatest and best Athenian of them all wearing a snub nose. Any physiognomist would have voted him least likely to succeed, and no matter what artist has ever depicted Socrates he has a snub nose.

One face-reader made a game recovery, and sluffed Socrates off as a sport of nature, the exception that proves the rule. That the snub nose is invariably impudent, the Athenian authorities, Hitler, and the Nixon White House would all agree, having been afflicted with it in the persons respectively of Socrates, Winston Churchill, and Dan Rather of the Columbia Broadcasting System.

The snub, round, flat, or fat nose (like Jove's) has not only Socrates and Churchill to its credit but also Rembrandt, Beethoven, Aristophanes, Copernicus, and Hannibal (and those Alps and elephants were no child's play). But God once didn't like snub noses (Leviticus XXI:18). While Jews, Christians, and Mohammedans (presumably in the nasal image of their conjoint maker) have noses one-third the length of their faces, only one-fourth the length of the Oriental face is wasted on the nose.

In any case, the snub nose has certain practical advantages. Indeed, Western Civilization was probably driven to invent kissing because its noses were so highly unsuited to lovey-dovey rubbings together. The Western nose is distinctly not snuggly and cuddly. Picture a pair of

Roman lovers in a parked chariot, or the back of an arena, whiling away the intermissions by rubbing aquiline noses while the stagehands changed Christians. You see at once that this is a distant relationship and a harsh encounter. Mouth-to-mouth osculation is obviously a vast improvement, although ancient Romans still required finesse and considerable puckering up.

The cogitative, or wide-nostriled, is a very serviceable nose, which is fortunate because it's what most of us have. Apparently all noses which won't fit into any other category are cogitative. So if you aren't Greek, Roman, Hawk, Celestial, or snub-nosed, you're cogitative. Active brains, lots of ideas, and analytic powers are available to us. (Ah, there's the rub. You have to work at it.) And the company could hardly be better. To name a few:

Chaucer	Molière	Descartes
Shakespeare	Michelangelo	Handel
Ben Jonson	Sir Isaac Newton	Bach
Goethe	Samuel Johnson	Galileo
Wordsworth	Talleyrand	

If it leans a little toward the Roman, you get also force and dignity; if toward the Greek, beauty.

Under cogitative, for lack of anywhere else to put it, goes the English nose, a logical outcome of having your country tramped over by ancient intruders from North, South, East, and West. A dash of Roman here. A bit of Celt there. And what you get when you add a touch of French sauciness to a Viking prow is difficult to describe. Sometimes the English nose comes out square on the end like Wordsworth's, or large and red like Ben Jonson's (reputedly not from ancestral invaders but from too much sack and too little sleep), or like Oliver Cromwell's, "a knob of oak." Fortunately, the frequently bulbous English nose takes well to ruddiness.

After all our research, the conclusion may be that if you want to be rich and famous, you probably have the right nose now, no matter how other people may regard it, beautywise. But times are changing. We are, in spite of Madison Avenue, developing a taste for reality. The mannequin male is gone; the doll-like woman is going.

But in any case, you've always had a nose fit for the gods, whose nasal endowment is richly varied. For example, gods in India have noses for all seasons. Vishnu, the Preserver, has a Greek nose; Brahma, the Creator, a cogitative nose; and Siva, a red, Roman nose. God, as portrayed by Italian Renaissance painters, has a commanding nose, which is fortunate because it is very difficult to look omnipotent while wearing a white nightgown several sizes too big which is about all they ever let him pose in.

The Blemished Life

*W*E CAN POSTPONE it no longer. We must now tangle with sexists—and antisexists—of both sexes. So far, we've managed to pussy-foot around the unpleasant fact that if you're destined to have a particular flaw, you'd better select your gender with great care. What is a flaw for the goose is not necessarily a flaw for the gander. And nowhere is that truth more apparent than on the skin.

Men and women may be, like Judy O'Grady and the Colonel's Lady, siblings under the skin. But on the skin, they're a different breed completely. Nobody, except teen-age boys with acne, cares much what a man's skin looks like. Richard Burton's pebbly hide fits well with a rugged masculine image. But transfer it to Elizabeth Taylor and it might have changed her whole acting career—not necessarily damaging it, perhaps even strengthening her roles, but many of them would probably not be the same roles.

Since time began, most cosmetics have been plastered, painted, brushed, or dusted onto women. Who knows why? Perhaps it's this: judged by the standards imposed on women, men have always looked dreadful. Maybe women are just hardened to it. Or maybe where the flesh is concerned, women have tougher sensibilities—and stronger stomachs. When you consider what the typical knight probably looked like shucked out of his shining armor after assorted jousting and other jolly blood-letting, you can see that delicate sensibilities would be no asset to lady fair.

Women have always been upchucked over by mewling infants, and confronted by billions of repulsive baby bottoms (a good many men would prefer a small brush with a grizzly bear to one with an exorbitantly utilized diaper). Women always nursed the most noxious diseases, bound up the most hideous wounds, and laid out the most revolting dead.

When her man crawled back to the cave, his skin ribboned by wild animals, or came courting with the proud mutilations of a Prussian duelist or a tribal brave, or returned maimed and disfigured from battle, a woman had to learn to look without flinching.

Or maybe women just had to put up with it because of their dependence upon their lords and masters; or couldn't be choosey because of the perennial shortage of men after wars or even epidemics, the male being more mortal than the female; or maybe (dare we say it) women are better at looking beneath the surface for the qualities they seek in a mate.

Anyhow, if you're coming down with a bad case of skin bumps, arrange to be a man and not a woman—or a teen-age boy. Otherwise, it's apt to make you feel bad—

even if you happen to be a Prince of Wales and can create a fashion of high collars and stocks so the scars on your neck will not show. George Augustus Frederick, son of George III, and slated to give his name to the elegant Regency period of England, was a brilliant, handsome prince, with (his description) "limbs well proportioned," his features, "strong and manly," his eyes, "grey and . . . though none of the best, passable." Yet he was bowed down with seventeen-year-old gloom because of pimples. The House of Hanover being particularly prone to tears, no doubt young George Augustus wept copiously over his affliction.

Of course, except for two or three stubborn plagues, skin is no longer a problem. The worst of the disfiguring diseases are gone forever (so long as we remember to keep inoculated), but in Elizabethan times, women had it very rough indeed. Their era combined smallpox with an absolute mania for perfect, alabaster skin. The pallor wasn't too difficult. You stayed out of the sun. When in it you wore large sheltering hats, and even masks for protection against the rude buffeting of wind and sun. Perfection was something else again.

Many an Elizabethan lady's alabaster skin had been deeply pitted by smallpox, especially if she had failed to hang a red petticoat across the window during the acute phase of the disease. So the first step in Elizabethan make-up was often puttying over the cavities. And what they puttied, sandpapered, smoothed, and painted with should make any present-day woman grateful to her corner drug-store, whose potions are comparatively benign, except for a bit of liver damage here or there from hair spray and the habits of spray cans whose every woosh costs her, and us, and unborn generations forever one more fraction of ozone from their air.

While the Elizabethan ladies were less destructive to the environment, they were exceedingly destructive to themselves. But Beauty made demands in those days that *Vogue* would never risk in its most supreme dicta. One must have a rounded face with high color, a high white forehead, small, penciled eyebrows, eyes "lamp like" (but modestly lowered), dimples, a snowy white round neck holding the head well up, round ears, and rich golden yellow hair.

The breasts must be high, round, and pale; the hand small, white, and red nailed; the hips large (and, if necessary, padded); the feet small with a high instep. All this was not easy to achieve.

The painting, plucking, bleaching, and plastering that went on was phenomenal. And their beauty recipes! (So unlike our own turtle oils, royal bee jellies, and ambergris—which if you don't know what it is, don't look it up. You're better off not knowing.) There was a powder made from burned jawbones of a hog, and a favorite formula that specified, "Take a young raven from the nest, feed it on hard-boiled eggs for forty days, kill it and distill it with talc, almond oil, and myrtle leaves." You could, of course, cure your blemishes by washing in the waning moon with elder leaves, distilled in the month of May. Even if it did nothing for your skin, you'd at least have had a beautiful experience.

The alternatives could be hellish: ground brimstone and turpentine; or Soliman, which like modern sandpapering really worked, taking off freckles, spots, warts, and other blemishes—along with the top layers of skin. Being sublimate of mercury, it also blackened the teeth and brought on the "shakes." A nice permanent high color could be achieved with red crystalline mercuric sulphide which ate into the flesh.

Since gowns bared the bosom, it too was whitened with thin blue veins neatly penciled on.

In other words, the noble Elizabethan ladies looked ghastly—scarred and painted like clowns—and not the least ghastly was Good Queen Bess. Fortunately, she had a fine tough constitution and lived through all her cosmetics to a ripe old age.

But cosmetics probably began, like almost all human adornment, not just to attract fellow humans but to titillate the gods with whom one thereby hoped to make advantageous deals like not being struck by lightning or turned to salt. Skin has a mystical import in the legends of many lands, not all happy. An ancient Norse legend said a magic carpet could be made from the skin of a corpse. And lest one think the Nazis had, in their lampshades, perpetrated a new obscenity, it can be pointed out that the French used human leather at least until the 18th century, and a British library has the proceedings of the murder trial of William Corder, executed in 1828 for "the murder of Maria Marten in the Red Barn," which were bound in leather prepared from the murderer's corpse by a West Suffolk surgeon. (The most horrible fact about the Nazis was that their obscenities were *not* new, just more efficient.)

But let us draw back from the inferno of inhumanity's repertoire with regard to skin, and go on to the very avant-garde civilization of ancient India. There, in the Sus'rata, one could find twenty-four rules for good health and preservation of bodily appearance, all carefully detailed: nail paring, hair care, tooth washing, and much wisdom on bathing and rubbing with oils. (Soap and water was one cosmetic the English and French courts rarely applied to the skin.) Here men used much the same make-up as women except for the elaborate paintings which decorated the cheekbones with flowers and animals (as in the sculpture pieces at Bhara). These, presumably, created a kind of facial puppetry, with animals leaping and crouching as one smiled or frowned. Not at all a bad item to have among one's make-up possibilities. Such a lovely way to hide blemishes, among flowers and leaves.

Some Indian women smeared themselves all over with wet clay before bathing. Worldly ladies used scented bath powders. Nuns, who seemed to get a raw deal in everything, could have only red clay and rice husks for their bathing, and definitely no steam baths for them. Probably they were not even allowed the pleasure of back scratchers made from crocodiles' teeth. These versatile reptiles (whose cosmetic properties have never helped their own beauty problems) show up again in the Middle Ages in Europe, where for centuries, crocodile excrement was used for mud packs.

The crocodile product was probably perfectly safe (gathering it may not have been!) at least compared to the white lead used in the Elizabethan and later eras. Lady Coventry, a vivacious leader of London society in the 1750s, died of lead poisoning from her make-up. Of course, many other women did too but Lady Coventry's fate held a special poignancy. Although she was renowned for her natural beauty, her husband insisted that she dramatize it with rouge and the other lead-based cosmetics that caused her death.

The itchingest man in history was a London society

doctor, Jean Paul Marat, who made three serious mistakes: he did not stick to fee-collecting but poked his nose
into politics; he frequented the drains and sewers of Paris;
and he was mean to some friends of a poor but noble
young lady of hot temper and steadfastness of purpose.
The first error landed him in the middle of the French
Revolution, a very bad place for the health. It wasn't safe
to belong to any side in the Revolution, but it was even
more dangerous to be a loner. Taking his liberté and éga-
lité without the fraternité finally got him chased into the
sewers of Paris. Unlike the sewers of New York which
(workers swear to this) are atwinkle with the bright eyes of
flushed-down alligators, the sewers of Paris had only rats
and germs. From these he caught a horrible relative of
dandruff called pityriasis simplex which made him itch so
bad that one cannot read the description without scratching. (You will be spared the details because neither can
one write the description without scratching.) It drove the
good doctor crazy, and he had to remain immersed in
warm water for relief. Fortunately, if your revolutionary
role is writing you can keep on being mightier than the
sword even from a bathtub. However, if you get a letter
from a girl in your home-town in Normandy, don't answer. "Citizen," the lady wrote, "your love for your native
place doubtless makes you desirous of learning the events
which have occurred in that part of the Republic. . . .
Have the goodness to receive me and give me a brief inter-
view. I will put you in a condition to render a great service
to France." (Oo la la, those Frenchies with their double
entendres, what!) When entertaining a citizeness in the
bath, instead of playful dalliance, he recited the list of revolutionaries he was sending to the guillotine this week.
However, he never checked first to see which side she was

on. Now most people can't stab themselves or anybody else in the heart because they haven't any idea where the heart is, but this physician had the bad luck to get a woman who knew her anatomy, or, rather, his. He got a dinner knife right to the aorta.

This seems to be a story with no losers. Jean Paul Marat got a merciful release from his itching, the whole government attended his funeral, his bust was put in a place of honor in the Assembly, there was a first-rate David painting of his assassination, and he was revered as a Friend of the People. Even his ashes were transferred to the Pantheon with great pomp. (Of course, they got thrown out the next year but *c'est la politique.*)

Charlotte Corday went, with utter calm, to the guillotine and to her otherwise totally unmerited place in history. All that the encyclopedias can find to say about her is that she lived with an aunt and read Voltaire and Plutarch—probably picking up ideas from the latter's gossip about Caesar and his friends, but, it must be said, vastly improving on them. If one compares those butterfingers, Brutus (*et tu*), Cassius (the scrawny one), and Casca (the boring one) and their clumsy daggering with Charlotte's cool dispatch, there's simply no comparison. They probably couldn't have carved a roast with a dinner knife.

So much for dandruff.

When Franklin Roosevelt was honeymooning in Italy in 1905, he had a problem about which he wrote to his family: "We are both flourishing but I have had hives for ten days and they won't go, so people think I have a flea that won't get killed by any method."

Fortunately he recovered. Otherwise, he could not be president of the United States. No blemishes for the presidential face. *The Presidents of the United States*, published by the White House Historical Association (and who should know if it doesn't?), portrays only two little bumps (both Teddy Roosevelt's) on the countenances of thirty-eight presidents, despite all the battles, smallpoxes, and Indian skirmishes they had survived. Famous men are no longer so fortunate; in fact, they are, dermatically speaking, deplorable. In *The Faces of Greatness* by the photographer Youssoff Karsh, among ninety famous men, we find, alas, thirty-five sets of moles, wens, warts, and other excrescences, from those of Albert Einstein to those of Christian Dior; thirteen lots of freckles and other dark spots, from Picasso to Thornton Wilder; twenty reminders of acne or other pimply pasts from Richard Rodgers to the Duke of Edinburgh. (In fact, Karsh may have achieved a royal first in portraiture. On the day he sat for Karsh, Prince Philip seemed to be sporting not one but two genuine pimples.) Albert Camus and Sir Thomas Beecham showed the scars of old injuries.

In fact, nothing could be cheerier than browsing through Karsh on a morning when one's mirror reflects an unusually discouraging array of bumps, blotches, and wrinkles. You may not have beautiful skin but there's obviously nothing to prevent it from becoming famous skin. Except, of course, you can't be president!

The exact truth is that the White House portraitists were, one and all, lying in their brushes. In fact, you'll be smart not to believe any formal portraits from cave paintings on, without the written text. George Washington's complexion ranged from rugged to dreadful, depending on the reporter. But even his loyalest fans, the Daughters of the American Revolution, concede that the surface of our hero was not much; a book not to be judged by its cover. His skin troubles began with smallpox in his socially embarrassed youth and added marks as he went from illness to illness and even to an ulceration of his cheek from lacerating dentures. Lincoln's quotation of Oliver Cromwell's instruction to paint him warts and all may have worked for Oliver, but apparently nothing can induce honesty in an American state portrait—so in the official picture of Lincoln, nary a wart.

Not only are candid pictures of famous people encouraging but, if you were to try to look at other people's faces from an eight-inch distance with harsh lighting it should bring happiness to your heart and sense to your head. Other people don't look too good in their bathroom mirrors either. And as you peer into their faces you could say, "It's all right. I'm just looking at your enlarged pores, blackheads, moles, warts, and general hickeyness, and believe me, madam, your skin is a mess." After all, why should you be more polite to other people than you are to your own reflection in the morning. Now, be honest, are the words you address to it tactful and courteous? Do you say, "Good morning, Face. I note you have a few pimples this morning but we'll fix those up and nobody will ever notice them. And if they do, what matter when they are on such a fine face belonging to such a desirable person."? A little palaver like that might be terribly good for your complexion as well as your morale. Cheer up the circulation, you know.

Somebody (who has been hated ever since) once said, "Sweet are the uses of adversity." But there has never been a better use of adversity than that of Josefina Guerrero in the Philippines, a woman of great value to her own country and to the United States because she had outstanding courage—and leprosy. She had had it for some time, but under wartime conditions proper treatment was no longer possible, and the lesions were clearly visible. (Leprosy is now under fair control; there are remedies; it is not very infectious at all, and the United States has numbers of people with well-controlled leprosy carrying on most of their normal lives among us.)

But it's one espionage gambit that even James Bond never thought of (although the Scarlet Pimpernel tried something close to it). Mrs. Guerrero was able to carry maps and messages through the Japanese lines with little difficulty. She made numerous trips, and when stopped by sentries, simply displayed the marks of leprosy and warned them not to come close. They passed her through quickly, showing no inclination to search. When the war ended, the grateful War Department brought Mrs. Guerrero to America for the most up-to-date treatment at the leprosarium in Louisiana.

There was once a United States congressman with leprosy but his story is not so uplifting. When his constituents understood (or rather failed to understand) the nature of his disease, they wouldn't vote for him anymore. Considering the number of moral lepers voters have put in office, one physical leper shouldn't have been any problem at all.

James Madison's problem was only a few malaria scars but that was serious enough. In order to compete for the presidency he needed something more heroic than evidence he had been felled by a mosquito. His opponent could boast of much bleeding and dying for his country, with much flaunting of the bloody shirt of Monroe. Madison's truthfulness cracked under the strain and he began to refer to his malarial aftermath as his battle scars. (He won, by the way.)

But unless you have some practical need for leprosy,

malaria, or acne, you will probably deplore any blemishes that mar your perfect alabaster hide, at least until you're famous enough for your blotches to turn into marks of greatness.

But how people feel about their blemishes depends upon many things. The school I attended had children with the Itch (scabies, an infectious disease caused by tiny parasites with a weakness for the warmth between the fingers). The worthier matrons of the town considered it a sure sign of filth, low morals and maternal slovenliness. When one day, my brother, on close inspection, was found to have succumbed, the leper was hastily scrubbed to a fare-thee-well, and annointed lavishly (like Napoleon) with sulphur and lard. He was then clapped between fresh sheets, and his clothes were carried off, at arm's length, to be stewed in a big boiler on the kitchen stove. (There seemed to be some maternal regret that the victim could not be safely sanitized in the same manner.) All this, while my mother tried to maintain a business-as-usual air lest I retail the family disgrace to schoolmates. Given no official briefing and, therefore, unsworn to secrecy, I relayed the rumor in traditional media fashion. The episode left an indelible imprint. When, decades later, I—now a great big grown-up psychologist—had a fingernail debilitated by a touch of psoriasis (a non-infectious, if incurable, disease), I knew that I was disgraced forever, this time there being no sulphur and lard to the rescue. Neglecting graver ailments, I pored over books of nutrition in search of magic potions, while inspecting the digit daily to the accompaniment of rising or lowering spirits. Either one of the placebos worked, or worry is a sure cure (or the disease just couldn't stand me), for the nail recovered and so did I.

Naturally, I am astonished when patients, who are *sup-*

posed to be neurotic, sometimes take even the Itch in their stride. One girl mentioned casually that she'd had something the doctors called scabies and it was a nuisance and also her boy friend had caught it from her. You see, she didn't know it was The Itch. I did not enlighten (or rather endarken) her, and glimpsed the benefits of not having had *my* mother, at least on the subject of skin. So do what your dermatologist tells you. Remember, your spots aren't a bit more impressive to other people than theirs are to you. (Others are, after all, just as narcissistic as you.) Furthermore, they've never stared at your imperfections in a bright light from eight inches away. But as somebody once said: there is no cosmetic for Beauty like happiness (and no psychologist will ever argue about that). Emotions and bodies make funny combinations. Losing your acne may make you more attractive. Losing your hang-ups about it certainly will. And once you're happier maybe the bumps will get discouraged and go away. I think acne has a weakness for unhappy teenagers.

And, of course, any woman who wants her skin to look its most radiant finishes her make-up with a kiss.

The Long, the Short, the Tall, and the Fat and Thin of It

O<small>NE DAY, NOT TOO LONG</small> from now, we will know how to make people any way we like. But when the mysteries of the gene are all unriddled, what size and shape would *you* have Brave New People be? All the same? At last, as in the dream of the Declaration of Independence, created equal? Then, no one will gain an unfair advantage because of his height and no one will ever again have to be distressed because of his lack or excess thereof—like poor George Washington, a man whose word you could trust on every subject but one, his size. On that subject he consistently lied in his teeth (both the real and the false ones). Apparently, he even deceived himself and his tailor, for his clothes more often fitted the size he wanted to be than the size he was. In a day when Virginians strove to retain the civility of English gentry while contending with the harsh realities of frontier life, a certain delicacy of body was much admired, even in men.

George's big hulk made him feel gauche and overgrown. He was indeed a very large man for his day. He said six feet but this seems to have been a bare-faced lie. The truth was he was at least six feet two inches, some said six feet six, and his body after death measured six feet three inches. So he was often too big for his breeches, not only in the eyes of the British but in the eyes of his own tailor. "I have hitherto," he wrote in discouragement, "had my clothes made by one Charles Lawrence in Old Fish Street. But whether it be the fault of the tailor or the measure sent, I can't say but certain it is, my clothes have never fitted me well. I enclose a measure and for a further insight, I don't think it amiss to add, that my stature is six feet; otherwise rather slender than corpulent." Even so, he was going to find the next lot didn't fit too well either. True, he was not corpulent but he did have a plump behind and a figure whose proportions were far from classical. In another letter to his brother Lawrence, he wrote, "You will take care to make the Breeches longer than you sent me last."

John Adams, whose manic-depressive cycles could have used lithium treatment ("sometimes absolutely out of his senses" was Benjamin Franklin's appraisal) was humiliated by his small size and much irritated by the tallness of Washington and Jefferson as well as by their more aristocratic backgrounds.

When Washington commanded the Revolutionary army, he tended to appoint large men to lead the various regiments. Perhaps he felt less conspicuous and overgrown among them. Fortunately for Ulysses S. Grant, *his* commander-in-chief, Abraham Lincoln, didn't give a damn how short a general was (or for that matter how much he drank) so long as he got results.

So George Washington might like the idea of a nation where each man was the equal of his neighbor in size and shape, and no more trouble with one's tailor.

But what size shall it be?

That's easy. Tall, muscular, well-proportioned men, and delicate, graceful women. Surely no one could object to that: nature at its best.

But the antisexists would object strenuously. Nature, they would say, had nothing to do with the smaller size of women. Male chauvinism did that to them. The sexes were probably once the same size (as they are approximately today among the Malays), but because of the physical frailty of men and their warlike propensities there were always more women than men, and the men, not having the courage to cope with women their own size, acted like wolves. They preyed on the weakest specimens of womanhood, the easiest to rape, abduct, brutalize into submission, and rule within the home. And this unnatural selection of small women for breeding has given us our present mismatched sizes which incites the male to chauvinism and perpetuates the oppression of women. We must return women to their natural size—as large and strong as men. I suggest Julia Child, television's French Chef, as the prototype of Brave New Female Personhood; she's fine, tall (6'3"), intelligent, amiable, and what's wrong with a world full of good cooks—so long, of course, as there are both males and females to do the cooking.

Agreed then, men and women both should be above average in size, but let's make them giants. It'll be easy to get government funds if we make them bigger and better

than the world has ever seen. We can probably get it right
out of the defense budget; the Pentagon will love the idea.
Of course, the tallest men in history, the ones over 8 feet,
have generally had runaway pituitary glands (like the
Roman emperor Maximus?). But we've had perfectly
healthy giants like 7-foot 9-inch Angus McAskill, the
Scottish giant who lived a hundred years ago.

And remember old Frederick William of Prussia's regiment of tall men, all over seven feet. The king was crazy
in lots of ways. He made his children's lives pure hell, and
he used his cane to break the noses and teeth of anybody
who offended him at home or on the streets of Berlin. He
collected tall grenadiers, over two thousand of them; the
tallest was eight feet three inches. His method as a collector made up in zeal for what it lacked in ethics and discre-
tion. His scouts were everywhere in Europe, coaxing,
buying, kidnapping, smuggling. One of his prize specimens was an Irish giant shanghaied from the streets of
London. This maneuver alone cost Frederick William
£1,000 in expenses. Once or twice he almost started wars
by his rapacity. Envoys wanting favors thoughtfully
brought a giant or two for the king's grenadiers. The Rus-
sians and Austrians were particularly generous. One Austrian ambassador, who happened to be extremely tall, was
seized one day by Frederick William's agents while alight-
ing from a cab in Hanover and almost found himself
added to the collection.

His tall soldiers were Frederick William's greatest comfort and joy. Having porphyria, the dreadful familial disease that drove his cousin George III equally, if less vio-
lently, mad, Frederick William was often ill and in
excruciating pain. At such times it cheered and consoled
him to have two or three hundred of his towering grenadiers marched through his bedchamber.

He liked small toy soldiers too and gave his little son Frederick (one day to be the Great) a platoon of small children, the Crown Prince Cadets. They were reviewed on a visit by Peter the Great and rewarded with a barrel of beer for good marksmanship.

While one would not have humanity copy Frederick William's frequently moronic giants, we could recommend a majestic or presidential height like Thomas Jefferson's or Chester Arthur's or Lyndon Johnson's. (We'd better not pick Washington because of his teeth and his low immunity to disease, always coming down with something lethal except during revolutions.)

But what about the environmentalists? Maybe we ought to consider them. If humanity were modeled after its smallest members, it would use up only half of the world's desperately scarce resources. Three-foot people would need only half as much food, clothing, and shelter. You could even have smaller space stations. Probably China, that model of efficiency, has already realized this and is busy planning midget-size Brave New Chinese. It's a marvelous idea and loads of models to choose from. History has many very tiny, very remarkable people. We could use somebody like Pauline Musters, for example, the smallest adult ever known to have existed. She was intelligent, fluent in four languages, and less than two feet tall, some said just a bit over one and a half feet, about as high as a six-foot man's knee. Think how far our natural resources would go for people her size. The subways wouldn't be crowded, the traffic wouldn't be snarled, every present apartment would be big enough for a triplex. We could laugh at the Arabs and their oil as we'd have plenty of our own if we were two feet tall. So let's run down the list of small people, and see what models we'd like to replicate.

There were two midget gods in ancient Egypt, but I suppose even science isn't yet up to making gods in its test tubes. And the first tiny human on record wasn't impressive. (He was merely a clerk in Egypt.) But Croesus certainly was. (He's the one you always say John Paul Getty, Aga Khan, and any Rockefeller are as rich as.) And Aesop certainly had a fabulous mind. Or there was Philetus of Kos, a poet and grammarian who tutored Ptolemy, the one whose system of astronomy almost got Galileo killed for disagreeing with it. They said Philetus was so small he wore lead shoes lest a puff of wind should carry him away. Alysius of Alexandria in the fourth century was only two feet tall, history says, but don't quite believe it. Very, very small people shrink in the telling and very, very tall ones stretch. Alysius was a Greek writer, thinker, logician, and philosopher. Cicero, the Roman orator, had trouble outdoing a rival speechmaker by the name of Licenius Calvus, so small he had to stand on a pile of turfs to bring him up to Cicero's height.

We'll skip over Attila the Hun, small enough to qualify but too horrid to contemplate. Even Pepin, the Short, king of the Franks and father of Charlemagne, is too bloodthirsty although he had enough strength and courage. Poland's great hero Wladislaus I, who reigned at the end of the thirteenth century, was a very small package of dynamic leadership, who by giant-size military, diplomatic, and organizational skills welded a whole nation out of its separate principalities. (He also swiped a couple of other countries for good measure.)

And there's Caracus, Saladin's tiny advisor in the twelfth century. It was once a whim of royalty to have very large and very small humans in their retinues, sometimes to their royal benefit, sometimes not. A Visigoth king was killed, in 548, by a dwarf feigning lunacy. Sir Jeffrey Hudson was tamer but not much. He was a captain of horse and a courtier in the service of Charles I of England, three feet nine inches in armor, the smallest knight in history. Once he took offence at the look on a large nobleman's face, challenged him to a duel of swords, and polished him off. For this he was exiled from the court. He was, also, jailed at the age of sixty for taking part in the Popish Plot of Titus Oates.

Perhaps we should turn to holier men such as St. Gregory of Tours. He led a busy life. Becoming bishop by popular acclaim at the early age of thirty-six, he made a deadly enemy of the king of the moment named Chilperic who had attained his position through the assassination of his predecessor. Gregory showed the greatest skill in protecting his town from both the Frankish king and the governor of Tours. He first aroused the king's rage by celebrating the marriage of Merovich and Queen Brunhilda (whoever she was, but presumably not Wagner's because his was blotto over somebody named Siegfried). The king waxed his wroth even more when Gregory refused to hand over Chilperic's own son, who had taken refuge from Papa's temper in the church sanctuary. Then Gregory was hauled in front of the Council at Berny for using abusive language about Queen Ferdegond, but either she merited it, he didn't say it, or he lied like a politician, because he was acquitted by his oath. After the death and presumably departure to hell of Chilperic, things became easier for the future saint and he could get a little serious writing done, like ten books of Frankish history in which he put up a saintly struggle to be fair to the departed king but didn't quite make it; seven books of miracles; twenty biographies of bishops, abbots, and hermits; a manual for knowing when to hold which services by studying the stars; a life of St. Andrew translated from the Greek; and the *Seven Sleepers of Ephesus*, translated from the Syriac.

He also traveled around France and Germany a great deal on church and diplomatic business. Between journeys, he governed Tours with great firmness, repressing riots, and reducing the monks and nuns to obedience, perhaps the most remarkable feat of all when one remembers that the clergy of that era make the Brothers Berrigan and other obstreperous priests of the 1960s look like a bunch of pussy cats. It is not known for which of these notable achievements Gregory received his heavenly Oscar.

Francis Zunega, a dwarf in the service of Charles V of Spain, was a literary person and a scrappy fighter. His wit was so barbed that he was exiled from court and finally stabbed to death because of it. Even a deathbed didn't stop his wise-cracking. A friend, Perico de Ayald, impressed by the solemnity of the occasion, asked the expiring man to pray for him in heaven. Zunega replied, "Okay, tie a string around my finger so I don't forget." He has also been remembered in history (in the Cronica Berbesca) for his persistence in trying to extract a gift of marten furs from Charles V, who promised and never delivered.

Le Petit M. Richebourg was a Loyalist spy during the French Revolution. He was a servant of the Duchesse d'Orléans at a time when the duchesse was frantic regarding the fate of her son Louis Philippe (in line for the throne if only the Revolution could be quashed). Richebourg persuaded a maid to wrap him in a baby blanket and carry him into Paris to the royal palace. He made several trips this way, smuggling military plans and other secret documents. While his primary object failed and the royal family went to its grim destiny, there were very nice fringe benefits for Le Petit M. Richebourg. He married his transportation and they lived happily together for sixty years.

A marriage arranged by British royal whim turned out far more happily than that of the queen who arranged it. Richard Gibson was a painter of portraits (along with Van Dyck and other notable artists) in the court of that illustrious collector of art, Charles I of England. The king apparently valued Gibson's work highly.

In addition to being an admired artist, Gibson was also one of Queen Henrietta Maria's favorite midgets. Jean Shepherd was another of her small favorites, and the queen, like a little girl playing with her dolls, thought it would be charming to arrange a grand court wedding between the two. The occasion was a miniature as beautiful as any Gibson had ever painted of the royal family, although not without its historic irony. The small bride and groom lived happily ever after with five nice children who had noteworthy careers in the arts and in the military, and who were very kind to their parents in their old age.

The Court which surrounded their wedding day dispersed to its assorted dooms of battlefield, scaffold, and exile. Queen Henrietta and her children lived as neglected poor relations of the king of France until the restoration of the monarchy to England.

But how about settling for a model like Jean Francois de Cuvilles, an extremely small man who lived in the first part of the eighteenth century and was a leading architect and designer of the rococo era. He was first architect and chief of the Corps of Engineers and Architects to their serene highnesses, the Electors of Bavaria and Cologne. Cuvilles designed, in addition to the usual royal edifices, theater exteriors and interiors, stage machinery, land-scapes, lakes, fountains, furniture, trophies, vases, hel-mets, books, statues, stoves, or anything else their serene highnesses might require—twenty-three books of designs, many of them executed. Cuvilles is, in fact, the father of modern interior design.

In Munich, the Pavilion in the Park Nymphenbur, the Palais Holstein (now the Episcopal Palace), and the little theater of the residence are his design. Outside Munich are his hunting pavilion of Falkenlest near Cologne, the Castle Wilhemsthal near Kasel, and the church at Shaflan, Haute Baviere.

His personal life seems to have been as felicitous as his work. Happily married (although something of a philan-derer), he fathered a brood of up-and-coming children. Jean Francois, Jr., followed his father as chief architect and it was he who published many of his father's books of designs.

When you can get all that in the smallest of bodily con-tainers why waste material on six-foot models?

But I suppose no matter what the merits of miniaturiz-ing the human race we'll have to phase the larger models out gradually. Otherwise, we leftover Gullivers would have as rough a time squeezing outselves into Brave New Lilliput as Wilt Chamberlain does folding himself to fit into ours. But let's move in that direction and choose the smallest model that fits neatly into our present world, say, between five foot and five foot six—just Mozart size. And what possibilities to choose from: Beethoven, Keats (five feet), Swinburne, and Whistler (and, for all I know, his mother too). There's Andrew Carnegie and Geoffrey Chaucer, Savonarola, Ibsen, and John Paul Jones, of whom it was said, "Moving with a pronounced dignity, he appeared to be a formidable figure," or Franz Schubert ("A very little man but a giant"). We have Thoreau and Oliver Wendell Holmes, Chopin, and Simon Bolivar, the South American freedom fighter; David Garrick, the great British actor whose genius on stage made his size seem exactly right; Watteau, the French painter of outsize landscapes; Lord Nelson and King Nebuchadnezzar, the "dwarf of Babylon"; Michelangelo (didn't look in the least like Charlton Heston), and Louis XIV, on his high red heels, under his tall wigs, compensating for the height nature didn't provide. We could use Nelson Rockefeller or Mario Andretti, who won the Indianapolis 500 seated on a special seat so he could see over the dashboard of his racing car. Of course, we wouldn't want them as hot-tempered and lethal as those matched-for-size duelists, Alexander Hamilton and Aaron Burr. But we've got presidential timber anyhow with the five-foot six-inch quartet of John Adams and his son John Quincy, James Madison and Martin Van Buren, although there has never yet been a very, very short holder of the presidency.

Oh, yes, the world could manage very well left to the talents of its smallest people. But whatever we choose, large or small, we will obviously want people with beautifully proportioned bodies—like Greek gods and goddesses.

We'll get a hard time from the efficiency experts on that one. You don't manufacture people for looks but for function and you'll find they'll look just right once you see them with a vision freed from stereotypes. Function is Beauty. Compare the beautiful lines of a Xerox machine with a Detroit Dreadful, all gussied up in cheap tin. Clean efficient lines, we say. You've probably never noticed just how inefficient most human bodies are, and such total anachronisms. They can't even stand upright like a good stable machine, they expend enormous quantities of energy just staying in one place and their center of gravity is not nearly low enough for good balance. And all that size and those old-fashioned muscles in a world where a four-year-old child and a machine can lift more than a thousand men. Useless muscles that have to be exercised like a race horse, in all kinds of silly, boring unproductive consumption of energy. Is that any way to build a machine?

Granted we've never sorted people according to size and shape and used them appropriately. (Except maybe basketball players and jockeys, and during World War II Lockheed needed welding done inside airplane wings and turned gratefully to midget-sized welders.) But mostly we've ignored our diversity or disparaged it instead of appreciating its possibilities.

Variation according to function will be the keynote. Now let's see what we will need. A few large, burly types for the unautomated, brute-force jobs that still remain. I suppose a very, very few tall slender ones for speed and reach, but they are, in general, a bad bet. They break too easily and the tall thin column is too unstable on its base, so we won't manufacture any more than we really have to. We'll standardize wherever we can on small sturdy sizes.

The executive model, for instance, will have a large head and seating area, slight musculature, long arms for desk work, much development and refinement of the chest and neck area for maximum voice efficiency, and reduction of all possible energy-consuming and sedentary stress areas. In fact, this will probably be the basic efficiency model for Brave New World for both men and women—a model that has no more muscles that can be fully exercised within the activities of a normal day, and large buttocks for sitting comfort, and large platform feet for standing around.

Men will need restyling essentially by miniaturizing and demuscling, while upgrading their sturdiness to a par with women in order to equalize their longevity. The female form poses a few questions, however. The wide bottom, now in some disrepute, but throughout most of history so alluring and desirable to the male, is no longer functionally necessary for dextrous childbearing because of perfected Caesarian operations, the relative infrequency of reproduction, and the probability that most infants will emerge through the neck not of a uterus but of a laboratory jar.

Breasts pose a particular quandary. From the efficiency standpoint they should be deleted. They are functionally anachronistic, prone to medical complications, a nuisance to hold up, and a red rag to the antisexists with their To Bra or Not to Bra. If you wear, you're turning yourself into a mere sex object to gratify and entice male chauvinist you-know-whats. You're denying the natural, untrammeled beauty of the form female. And you're getting mutilated by shoulder straps and steels. If you don't wear, all the antisexists with neat, buoyant bosoms may run rings around you with the aforesaid male you-know-whats. Your clothes are going to look like hell no matter how bravely you insist mother hubbard drapes are so beautiful, so authentic.

Better to eliminate the whole issue—so no more breasts. The seemingly inconsolable *Playboy* crowd will soon get over its fetish for mammary gigantism and revive the lecherous instincts of its 1920s grandfathers who went wild over Centerfold Flat. But these are details that can be worked out.

One would think a dozen varieties of human ought to fill the bill, although we'll have to custom-make an occasional concert pianist or something like that.

In theory, the efficiency expert is, of course, perfectly right. People should be the right size and shapes for the work to be done, and beauty can be safely ignored. Whatever is utilitarian will soon seem beautiful, just as skyscrapers of glass (and what looks like black tar paper) have come to seem more beautiful to many than the ornate old buildings that we no longer have the money or the craftsmanship to make. After all, how do you think the present human form would look to you if the first one you'd ever seen had been two or three inches long and found under an overturned rock? So, no serious esthetic problems should be involved.

But maybe it's not nice to fool around with Mother Nature. She might get mad and carry on about it: You meddling fools, she'd say, you nincompoops, you machine heads. Don't you understand. It's not beauty, or conformity, or efficiency but sheer, wonderful, profligate variety that's the wealth of humanity. Even you, humans, with your dull conforming and your stupid stereotypes. I'm telling you, even you are going to be bored with your assembly-produced people. Can't you see how you make the biggest, most fascinating tapestry in the world? Who wants all the pictures in the world to be Rembrandts or Da Vincis? My god, you'd make a million identical twins. A hundred thousand Garbos. Oh, no! But I suppose you'll have your fling. You usually do. And Nature will have to clean up after you. It usually does. But try it my way once. Put in the ingredients and let them combine as they will. Then watch and see what comes of it.

Why can't you take people like packages under a

Christmas tree, not knowing what gift is inside. Variety and mystery, that's the thing; thin, thick, long, short, sharp, soft, with all kinds of intriguing bulges and the excitement of trying to guess from the outside what's inside; what kind of person lives or hides within. A few things you're sure of right away. If the person comes in a large bodily container, it's not a jockey; if it's five feet long, it's probably not a football player; if it's bulky, it's not an airline stewardess (they're not allowed to get fat) or an ancient Spartan (they were fined if they did).

Aside from a few such exclusions, your guesses about the contents of human packages aren't too good, although a psychologist by the name of Sheldon has it all worked out to his satisfaction (other psychologists mostly yawn and say, "Yeah, yeah, maybe"). According to Sheldon, if you're tall and scrawny, an ectomorph he calls it, you're likely be scholarly and ascetic. (This means, I think, that you only get turned on by lush females if you find them in Greek poetry or something like that.) He says if you're a plumpish endomorph, you go in for creature comforts rather than mental effort or bar bells. (Good thinking there, Chief. If you're plumpish, it's quite probable you *have* gone in for creature comforts.)

But there have been a good many fat thinkers and philosophers who have upset Sheldon's theories by having great appetites to match their great minds. David Hume, the Scottish philosopher, was even philosophical about his avoirdupois. "I cannot," he said, "but bless the memory of Julius Caesar for the great esteem he expressed for fat men and his aversion to lean ones."

Dr. Erasmus Darwin, grandfather of two great British scientists, Charles Darwin and Sir Francis Galton (and in some ways outreaching the scope of even their illustrious minds), was enormously fat. (And urged his patients to eat plentifully, especially of sweets.) Although he had a disapproval of liquor much deplored by his friends, he enjoyed his creature comforts like the most sybaritic of Sheldon's endomorphs. But there is, says his biographer and descendant, Hesketh Pearson, "hardly an idea and hardly an invention in the world today that he did not father or foresee, from the philosophy of Mr. Bernard Shaw to the phonograph of Mr. Thomas Edison, from eugenics and evolution to airplanes and submarines, from psychoanalysis to antiseptics. He founded the Lunar Society—the most remarkable group of thinkers and inventors of the eighteenth century—which had a more patent effect upon civilization that that of any other society in history. He was the greatest English philosopher and physician of his day [and a much acclaimed poet to boot]. He was a notable humanitarian and reformer, centuries ahead of his time, and, rarer still, an extremely benevolent and reasonable human being."

Not only was he extremely fat, but he had a clumsy gait and an "unrefined face" with smallpox marks, and he sometimes walked with his tongue hanging out. He stammered abominably. (When asked by a young man if he didn't find the stammering very inconvenient, Dr. Darwin replied, "No, sir, it gives me time for reflection and saves me from answering impertinent questions.") But not only were his words worth waiting for, his company was so stimulating that intellectuals to this day could envy the members of his society of "Lunatics." Since neither Erasmus Darwin's speech disorder nor his prodigious fat precluded an exceedingly rapid rise to social, medical, and scholarly eminence, he seems very sensible not to have wasted self-pity or disapprobation upon them. (Or is that cart before horse? Maybe it didn't impede him because he refused to fuss himself about it.)

He rarely had the slightest trouble attracting women, and was married twice, first to a "blooming and lovely young lady of 18." After she died, he fathered two illegitimate daughters whom he openly acknowledged, educated, and often entertained in his home. In middle age, he tumbled head over heels into love with the wife of a neighboring colonel, and lapsed into melancholy and poetry over this lady, "in the full bloom of her youth and beauty." Fortunately her "peevish and suspicious" husband died, but even so all was not smooth sailing. All the eligible young men in the district were also courting his lady love, and the competition was fierce. She was surrounded by "rivals whose time of life had nearer parity with her own, yet in its summer bloom, while his age approached its half century; whose fortunes were affluent . . . ; who were jocund bachelors, while he had children for whom he must provide." (By this time, he was also lame.) The lady herself stated firmly, "He is too old for me."

But Dr. Darwin outdistanced the field and won the prize. The apparently incongruous couple seems to have been extraordinarily happy. Their bevy of children cherished the happiest memories of their childhood; the doctor sharing their fun and festivities and showing himself as clever at instant nonsense verse as he was at everything else.

With all Dr. Darwin's prevision of the future, he never would have believed the plight in which fat people would find themselves in the twentieth century. That one should be chastised for a goodly corpulence and not only submit to the chastisement but chastise oneself over any natural bodily state would outrage his independent spirit and his compassionate heart. One shudders to picture him confronted by a Weight Watchers meal instead of a luncheon table "set out with hothouse fruits, West India sweet meats, clotted cream, Stilton cheese," and many other succulent dishes.

When making house calls, Darwin usually sat down to a good meal before entering the sickroom, not only to indulge the inner physician but also, by his leisurely approach, to allay the fears of the worried relatives.

While Dr. Darwin was stowing away cakes and assorted other cholesterol traps for health, pleasure and his image as poet, scholar, benign physician and jovial friend, his contemporary and fellow poet, Lord Byron, was dieting on cold potatoes and vinegar, biscuits and soda water to maintain his image. Dieters will be discouraged to remember that Byron died at thirty-six, Dr. Darwin at seventy-one.

Rudolph Valentino, as a struggling young dancer at Maxim's in Paris, handled his weight problem somewhat differently. He had never eaten so well in his underprivileged life and could scarcely be coaxed out of the kitchen long enough to dance. Yet Maxim's dancers had to remain very slender. Valentino soon had to choose between his stomach and his job. Fortunately, he found a way of eating his cake and not having it show. He donned a corset.

While Darwin foresaw psychoanalysis, he did not expect it to be the bane of fat people with its postulation that if you are overweight it's probably a sign you're fixated at the oral level, that is, at the breast (or the nursing bottle as the case may be) rather than having your mind on sex like they say it ought to be. Dr. Darwin himself managed apparently to attend well to both bodily needs. Anyhow, the latest flash on overweight suggests maybe it wasn't you but your mother that was fixated at the oral level, causing her to overstuff you in infancy, thereby giving you a surplus of fat cells that kept on having to be richly fed.

Researchers themselves seem to have a fixation on fat women and sex, their notion usually being that if you're overweight and female, you'd rather eat than have sex. However, the latest flash (out of Chicago) is that fat wives like sex even oftener than thin wives.

A Dr. Friedman advocates sex with your food, pointing out that sex uses up calories in healthful exercise and hopefully unfixates your mind from the refrigerator door. As he puts it in a jolly slogan, "Reach for your mate instead of your plate." He does not say whether it is advisable to confide to your mate that he or she is is a new version of Metrecal.

Not that fat isn't a great nuisance. For example, if you're a ruler in the Middle Ages, you're sure to have offended God—plenty and often—and, therefore, before an eyeball-to-eyeball confrontation with St. Peter it is prudent to make a pilgrimage to Jerusalem, or, at least, to Rome as spectacular proof of your basic piety. In those days you could put anything over on the Lord; you could rape and pillage all the way there and all the way back so long as you made it to the Holy Sepulchre. Now, Elector John of Brandenberg undoubtedly needed shriving as much as the next one, but he had a problem. He couldn't even get to Rome because he was so fat he could not mount his horse. He, therefore, commanded his physicians to cut a large amount of fat from his stomach. The physicians didn't do it but we trust the Recording Angel gave him an M for Motivation.

George II of England, who came of a long line of inbred fat German princes and princesses, probably had an extremely large number of fat cells and, according to the newest theories, should have reconciled himself to being one more plump Hanoverian monarch. But unlike most of his ancestors and his descendants, who ate lavishly, this George was so determined to keep a slim, princely profile that he almost starved himself.

William the Conqueror, long after he had presented centuries of schoolchildren with that hopefully memorable date, 1066, and all that, became corpulent and unwieldy. Philip of France laughed at stout William for being so womanish as to go to a medieval reducing resort. This made the Conqueror so mad that he set out to sack and burn Paris. That city has always had a penchant for hair-raising escapes from potential sackers (including Hitler), and was saved presumably by divine providence, this time in the form of a gopher hole or some French equivalent. William's horse stumbled, heaving him against the pommel of his saddle, causing injuries so severe that he died from peritonitis within a few days—but only after reflecting upon his sinful past and giving instructions for reparations to his victims. He even let his odious half-brother Odo out of prison, but whether that was racked up on the debit or credit side of the heavenly ledger is debatable.

President Taft's problem was the White House bathtub. Designed for lesser men, it was far too small for him and he got stuck in it several times. He finally had a special one constructed, big enough so you could have scrubbed John Adams, John Quincy, James Madison, and Martin Van Buren all at the same time. He tried a variety of reducing methods, once by riding a great deal—which apparently exercised the horse more than Taft. In 1905, an English physician put him on a Spartan diet and he went down from 326 to 250 pounds. Since he loved food and his favorite dishes were lobster newburgh, the recipe for which called for a cup and a half of thick cream, and chicken croquettes with a pint of light cream, it will not surprise you—or anyone who has ever dieted—to know that the weight went right back on.

Once President Taft went to the mountains to recuperate from amoebic dysentery. Secretary of War Elihu Root, having inquired of the president's health, received the following telegram: "Stood trip well, rode horseback 25 miles to 25,000 foot elevation." Root wrote back, "Referring to your telegram. How is the horse?"

Whether Henry VIII's courtiers were being tactful, currying favor, taking out a little extra life insurance, or just following a fashion set by the king isn't precisely known, but as Henry's girth increased, so did theirs—with pillows. Fortunately, President Taft's cabinet felt no need to follow this courtly example, and the president himself seemed relaxed about his extravagant poundage and outsize appetite.

It is rough if one is an undesirable size and also happens to be a child. Adults are at least polite to one another's faces. Between parents pointing out one's over- or underweight condition and pestering about eating or not eating, and the ungraciousness of one's peers, children's spirits may be permanently dampened.

Andrew Jackson was as unprepossessing and unpromising a lad as you'd be likely to find. At 13, he was tall, skinny, freckled, and had not yet grown out of a tendency to drool when he talked, especially when he got excited—which was pretty often, because if taunted, he could be depended on to fly into a rage which was great fun to his tormentors, especially if they happened to be at a safe distance. This is thought to be one source of his lifelong toughness when slighted, defied or insulted.

Wherever he came by his hot and sometimes vicious

temper, he was also capable of extraordinary love and tenderness. Jackson could never resist small children, and there were always some living at the White House. The children's parties were the best ever, and whenever their parents needed a babysitter, the president was delighted to oblige. One presidential conference had to be delayed because the president was found holding a sleeping two-year-old who could not be disturbed. He is known as Old Hickory, but he might with equal justice have been remembered as Old Softie.

Washington was an overgrown young man (in an age of ultra-refinement), and socially clumsy. But unlike many adolescents who feel awkward and self-conscious, he showed a hero's true colors. He kept right in there pitching, asking the ladies to dance; and when they got to know him, George turned out to be very good company, an amiable lad who loved a good time.

You might think a young cavalry officer who was known as the Little Beauty of the Regiment might be due for a difficult career. He was light and weak and always needed too much sleep. He probably had a latent case of TB. He had a soft, pretty, girlish face with a rosy complexion, small delicate hands, and a soft, melodious voice. He was ridiculously modest (perhaps ashamed of his male accoutrement) and would never bathe along with the other recruits. He was a soldier who couldn't stand the sight of blood or injured animals, and couldn't touch meat unless it was almost burned. He only cursed once (when somebody mistreated his horse) and never raised his sword if he could help it. His military career was as poor as one might predict except, of course, for winning the Civil War. He and his wife are buried on a pleasant hill overlooking the Hudson River, in Grant's Tomb.

Boys who don't look too good at this moment can take comfort from Thomas Jefferson, who was a skinny, homely kid. As somebody put it, "most unattractive in his youth but good looking at maturity and beautiful in age"—by general agreement, a handsome president.

Abraham Lincoln didn't even have a good-looking maturity to look forward to. Gawky he was in the beginning and gawky he remained, probably because of something called Marfan's Disease, which abnormally lengthens the bones. When Nancy Lincoln let Dennis Hanks hold his newborn cousin, warning him, "Be careful, Dennis, fur you air the fust boy he's ever seed," the baby set up such a caterwauling that Dennis hastily relinquished the infant, saying, "Aunt, take him! He'll never come to much." (And appearance-wise, Abe never did.) At fourteen, he stood almost 6 feet 4 inches, "the ganglin'est, awkwardest feller that ever stepped over a ten rail fence; he 'peared to be all j'ints."

His stepmother didn't complain about Abe tracking mud over her floors. She could reach those. But she asked him to wash his hair so he wouldn't get the ceiling dirty, whereupon Abe found some small boys, waded them through a mud puddle, turned them upside down, and walked their muddy feet across the ceiling. His stepmother laughed till she cried and told him he should be spanked, and he cleaned the ceiling. By general agreement, Abraham Lincoln was the ugliest of American Pressidents—and, to many, the most beautiful.

Since there's clearly no way of deciding what size and shape we ought to be in, we might as well relax and enjoy the shape we are in. What you see in the mirror may be the dream of the test tube baby-makers of the future, the ideal model for all humanity!

Great Aches
and Pains

*A*s WE DESCEND into the contentious, even cantankerous, world of the medical history buff to tackle some famous gut issues, the reader will be wise to take them with a grain of bicarbonate of soda. The only thing a bunch of doctors argue about more than a live patient is one that's been dead three thousand years. Take Akhnaton, Great Pharaoh of Egypt, believer in the one true God. Scientist-historians have had a field day with Akhnaton. They have so far unearthed the following information regarding his physique: he had abnormally long bones because of acromegaly (not true, he had perfectly normal bones); he had rickets (he had not); he was an epileptic (he was not an epileptic); he had been castrated in his youth while a slave in the Sudan (he had never been in the Sudan, and in any case he couldn't have been a eunuch because he was really a woman). He was also the father of six daughters.

Some of these findings were badly shaken when it was discovered that his mummy was not his but somebody else's, namely his brother-in-law Amenhkara's, whom we would, therefore, suspect of being a very tall female eunuch with epilepsy, except that many of the diagnoses were made not from the family mummy but from bas-reliefs and statues. They may, therefore, reflect not only Akhnaton's anatomical peculiarities but also those of the artist. We project our own body images into our drawings, and if you should ever fall into the hands of a psychologist, you may be asked to make drawings, from which he will deduce a number of things—but hopefully not that you are an epileptic, a eunuch, or, unless you happen to be one, a woman. The historians, of course, may also be projecting *their* assorted anatomical problems onto the Great Pharaoh, whose name isn't really spelled Akhnaton but Iknaton and that isn't his original name anyhow, it being Junior (Amenhotep IV). That is, if it wasn't Irving or Moishe.

An exceedingly crudite internist of my acquaintance has been deciphering the ancient hieroglyphics, having learned the language to pursue hotly his theory that Akhnaton, Ikhnaton, Amenhotep or Nathan was actually a not-so-nice Jewish boy making good in Egypt and taking his Hebrew God with him. This theory has so far not won much acceptance in Egypt but, if my friend is as good at diagnosing the dead as he is at diagnosing the living, I may just go with it.

But be careful. This stuff is addictive and unless you read very gingerly *you* may find yourself mainlining Sanskrit or embroiled in the controversy over Napoleon's hemorrhoids, and did they or did they not lose him the Battle of Waterloo. Napoleon, an avid history buff, who, if he had been rich enough for advanced study, might have become a college professor and not an emperor, must have remembered his predecessor Charlemagne with envy. That remarkable conqueror and promoter of civilization in a Dark Age was tall and handsome with golden, perfumed hair and hardly a sick day in his life, just a little fat on the stomach in middle age and the need to rise in the night to relieve himself. Poor Napoleon, whose afflictions read like the plagues of Egypt, naturally had those too. Every night his bladder woke him several times. This sometimes made him very sleepy in the daytime, even in the middle of his biggest battles. He was drowsy before the gates of Moscow and again at Ligny. (Tactful—or squeamish—historians wrote of "his mysterious illness.")

With all the other torments of a Russian winter, the cold climate overloaded his kidneys, because he did not sweat enough. The confrontation of French and Russian armies at Borodino had to be delayed for two days out of respect for the emperor's kidneys. Even so, he became acutely ill an hour before the battle—not only in his kidneys but with a cough and acute laryngitis. (He had to scribble his orders as the battle raged.)

His wife, Josephine, once lost a battle of her own, one with which, unlike Napoleon's, we can all sympathize. One evening in the theater of the Palace of St. Cloud, in the middle of the first act, she was seized by an urgent need to urinate. She held out bravely, but unwisely, until the act was over, and then ran squirming to the small anteroom furnished with a chamber pot for such emergencies. Alas, no pot. While a messenger raced to correct the omission, the situation became terminal. Her ladies in waiting, like a circle of covered wagons, clustered around the empress to protect her from view. Josephine dropped her cashmere shawl on the parquet floor and soon felt much better. By this time she and her ladies were all helpless with laughter. An equerry arrived from Napoleon with the imperial order to "shush" but Josephine's laugh reflex was under no better control than her bladder. And what does a chamberlain do when he stoops to pick up milady's shawl and place it over her shoulders and finds it very damp? Why, he stuffs it in his pocket, of course. Apparently court and government life was hard on rank-and-file bladders too, for a minister in Paris warned a new appointee that because of the irregularity of his hours, in three months he too *"n'serez plus foutu de pisser."*

In addition to his bladder, a series of unimperial flaws plagued Napoleon, although his epilepsy was in the highest tradition—precedents having been set by Alexander the Great and Julius Caesar. Although, in Napoleon, it led, as things were wont to do, to the theater of the absurd. He had invited a very popular, very young actress, Mlle. George, to the palace for a night of bedtime frolic. Unfortunately, in the middle of the fun, he had a seizure. The young lady screamed with all her trained expertise. When Napoleon opened his eyes again, there staring down at him was a large contingent of the royal household— including Josephine. Napoleon promptly discharged the lady for hysteria under fire and neither Mlle. George nor her emperor had the slightest wish to ever meet again.

And naturally he caught the Itch. Scabies was very common at all levels of this phenomenally unwashed society (although Napoleon himself had the weird custom of taking baths). The Empress Marie-Louise had scabies as a young girl. The rich went to sulphur springs, the poor settled for a pot of sulphur ointment (the going remedy to this day). The discovery of its parasitic origin, in 1687, was regarded as heresy and hastily forgotten for another 150 years till an itchy medical student in Paris discovered it again. So while Napoleon didn't know what caused his scabies, he did know what to do for it. And meanwhile, he could be comforted by knowing that the itch was a sure cure for several other diseases including tuberculosis and epilepsy (didn't do a thing for Napoleon's). But before he got rid of it, he'd given it to Josephine, who was inclined to take a dim view of his shortcomings and complained loudly about this gift.

Much worse were recurrent bouts of neurodermatitis, which annoyed him at anxious periods of his career, although the scratching endeared him to his soldiers, giving them a warm companionable feeling as they itched their way across Europe. (The army that itches together, conquers together?) At least they sang as they scratched.

> The Little Corporal took such care of me,
> That no other could match him in generosity,
> He only took my hand as he promised me a post,
> And right off the bat, of the itch I can boast.

The soldiers in the trenches of World War II came to regard their affliction in much the same way. When they lay in hospital or convalescent center, clean, bathed, and itch-free, they sometimes played a game called Cootie in honor of the ubiquitous little creatures to which they had formerly given board and lodging.

But Napoleon's (and perhaps France's) Waterloo was hemorrhoids. Constipated all his life, he had had hemorrhoids for a long time. At the Battle of Ligny, he had been forced to ride all day with prolapsed and thrombosing piles, and as a result he had been too prostrated to follow up on his advantage. While Napoleon was being treated and gathering his strength for the next move, the British were busily deploying themselves in a better position on the fields at Waterloo.

In spite of his rest and treatment, on the morning of the battle Napoleon was still extremely tired. After breakfasting with his generals, he napped, waking at eleven, just half an hour before the first shots were fired. All day he was in severe pain and could scarcely be in the saddle at all. In the midst of the action, he retreated to his tent where the physician worked frantically to reduce the discomfort, but he was noted by those around him to be lethargic and the battle proceeded largely without its once-brilliant general.

In *his* day, Charles V of Spain had been wise enough to quit while he was still ahead. Once incredibly strong, "sagacious and versatile of mind," sovereign to Spain's great explorations of the New World, Charles came to grief from the family affliction—gout. By thirty the attacks were severe, and when the disease rendered him, in his own estimation, neither able to enjoy his kingship nor carry it on satisfactorily, he abdicated to a retirement of "mending clocks, watching a small estate, and receiving local nobility."

His son Philip II (of the Spanish Armada), remembering his father's fate, had his physician sit beside him at meals lest he forget his gout and overindulge.

Charles II of England, of the spaniels, Nell Gwyn, and bevies of other beautiful mistresses, also had a lusty appetite for food. This gave him sundry health problems, including diarrhea. At one meal of which we have the record, he ate four dishes of soup, a pheasant, a partridge, a heaping plate of salad, a large portion of mutton with garlic sauce, two large slices of ham, and a plateful of cakes topped with fruit and preserves. He also drank a lot. Because he had many gaps in his teeth, he often gulped his food without chewing. And the unfairness of it all! *He* never got fat or even very gouty.

Gout has often been the just dessert of glutton and gourmet. Monarchs with the most superb chefs were, of course, the most tempted; the rich and the noble hobbling close on their heels. A historical list of gout sufferers reads like an only slightly abbreviated *Almanac de Gothe,* for few kings and lords have had the exemplary self-control of Admiral Nelson. When good eating (with the Hamiltons, probably) caught up with him, he very sensibly went on a vegetarian diet for two years and cured it.

And Charles might never have been king except for Oliver Cromwell's bladder stones which interfered with his management of England after his successful revolution against the monarchy of the Stuarts. Anyone who has ever endured the distress of a bladder stone can sympathize. It is almost unbearable to think of the misery of those who lived before modern surgery and painkillers.

Samuel Pepys had his stone removed in an event so horrendous that he celebrated March 26 for many years as a feast day "for my cutting of the stone." To forestall further stones, he took turpentine and carried a rabbit's foot. Neither worked too well, turpentine being a notorious urinary irritant and the rabbit's foot proving defective and having to be replaced. His surgery had a very convenient complication. It had, asserted Mr. Pepys, made him physiologically incapable of restraining himself with a luscious female. So if caught making love to the serving wench (and he was), how could his wife blame *him!*

The nineteenth century was remarkable for powerful brains and weak stomachs. Its star thinkers covered reams of paper with harrowing details of their wayward innards, as they journeyed on to their ripe old ages. Thomas Carlyle, the great historian, accustomed to expressing himself in multiple volumes (five on the life of Frederick the Great), never skimped on hyperbole when describing his dyspepsia. He was, he said, bilious, yellow, and an insomniac, his distress "like a rat gnawing at the pit of his stomach." Since his doctors were dosing him with mercury powder (*we* worry about an occasional can of tuna), castor oil, and salts, his complaints were probably justified, although he said water taken as a medicine was the most destructive drug he ever tried. Despite his ailments, his home remedies, and his assortment of physicians, Carlyle lived to be thrown by a horse at seventy-three and to expire at eighty-five.

After his death, an article in the *British Medical Journal*, November 1895, concluded that Carlyle's sufferings were fully accounted for by the fact that he was particularly fond of "very nasty gingerbread." An eye specialist said it had all been astigmatism.

Young Charles Darwin had palpitations and pain around the heart at the thought of embarking on the *Beagle* for a scientific expedition in order to study the flora and fauna of the Galapagos, Tahiti, Australia, Tasmania, Brazil, and the Azores. Once on board, he exchanged palpitations for sea sickness and for the whole five-year voyage, he was ill much of the time, while he collected data and began to reinvent the history of man on earth. If the nineteenth-century world had foreseen the consequences to its peace of mind as a result of young Darwin's voyage, it might have had palpitations to match his own.

Darwin's internal miseries from the voyage set off a lifelong siege of ill health. For two days and two nights before his wedding, he had such a bad headache, "I doubted whether it ever meant to go and allow me to be married." Company gave him violent shivering and vomiting attacks. As a friend explained, "although strong enough corporeally he cannot stand mental fatigue and must have silence after dinner." Darwin considered it an unusually good day when he could write for two or three hours reclining on a couch. Because working made him so ill he decided "the facts [of ill health] compel me to conclude that my brain was never formed for much thinking." Since the thinking he did do revolutionized biology, turned the intellectual world upside down, shook the Christian religion to its foundation, and made his name a household word, one prefers not to think what might have happened if his health had been good. Just the same, one is glad to know that at the age of sixty he pepped up and felt much better until his death at seventy-three.

Thomas Huxley, another great biologist, whose insides were no better than Carlyle's or Darwin's, at least managed to be funny about them. When very young, maybe thirteen or fourteen, he had taken his first postmortem examination. After three hours bending over the corpse, he was doubled up with acute stomach paroxysms, severely poisoned by fumes from the embalming fluid. On that day he acquired "his constant friend, hypochondriacal dyspepsia," which "commenced its half century of co-tenancy of my fleshly tabernacle." This ailment soured his outlook on life, he said. "I am convinced that the Prophet Jeremiah must have been a flatulent dyspeptic—there is so much agreement between his views and mine."

These avant-garde thinkers often admired avant-garde medicine, which has not always been wise. Royalty, of course, has usually been blessed with illustrious medical practitioners—or cursed, since the correlation between fame and competence was sometimes low. The struggle of Queen Victoria's father for survival against his physicians' bloodletting, blistering, and general torturing is a sorry page of medical history. (He lost.) In the reign of James II, the royal pediatrician decreed that milk was a most noxious poison for any sickly infant. Only one of James' much-longed-for infant sons survived this edict.

Immanuel Kant, great German philosopher and one of the most important of modern thinkers, had been cagier than his English successors, and taken his health care firmly into his own hands. A tiny frail man with a hollow chest and hunched back, full of food allergies, he set up a most careful health regime and an absolutely rigid daily schedule. For example, when he took his long walks, he went alone (followed, however, by a servant with an umbrella, in case of rain). He reasoned that if he had a companion with him, he would talk. If he talked, he would breathe through his mouth. If he breathed through his mouth, he would chill his lungs, inviting coughs, sore throats, and pneumonia. Kant was also phobic about sweating, regarding it as even more dangerous than breathing. He also feared that garters would impede his circulation, and invented elaborate, but not very successful, devices to take their place.

And Immanuel Kant would never have permitted himself the slightest risk of dying of love, as a good many other people probably did, the air being full of lethal germs eager to cooperate with the slightest depression of physiological functioning. One always had friends generously sharing their TB bacilli or, failing that, one could tie into the going epidemic of smallpox, typhoid, or diphtheria; or one could escalate a few sniffles into pneumonia.

In our day, one is, alas, firmly affixed to life by antitoxins or antibiotics no matter how dilapidated one's spirits. Death of Grief isn't even an official category anymore in a coroner's reports. (We still have two or three illnesses thought to be precipitated by loss of love, but the range is so small and unpleasant they're hardly worth considering.) Back in the good old days, everybody seemed to be dying for love or at least considering it (except, of course, Immanuel Kant). John Keats was probably speeded on his way to an early grave "before high piled books, in charact'ry, held like rich garners the full-ripened grain," by the delectable Miss Fanny Brawne's callous disregard of her ailing poet.

And when the dashing Lord Ponsonby's wife discovered his long liaison with Harriette Wilson, the highest fashion courtesan of the day, and restored milord to marital fidelity, Harriette, who doted on him, lay face down on the floor praying to die. As the days wore on and her love did not show, she often fainted and had to be bled. The Duke of Wellington kindly rescued her from the financial straits into which her lover's defection had thrown her but could do nothing for her heart. As a lover, the great hero of Waterloo cut a poor figure in Harriette's eyes, looking "rather like a rat-catcher," she said in her famous, lively, *and* blackmailing *Memoirs*. When the Iron Duke was offered omission from the tome for a price, he stood up to her quite as well as he had to Napoleon. "Publish and be damned," he snorted. But compared to Ponsonby, "the handsomest man in all England," any man might have looked like a rat-catcher to poor Harriette. His beauty had indeed saved his life during the French Revolution. When the Parisians, offended by all Englishmen, caught him and dangled him from a lamppost in the Rue

St. Germain, women ran to cut him down because he was "too pretty a youth to die."

Harriette, whose standards in these matters were high, having surveyed at very close range England's bravest and the best, or, at least, its richest and noblest, had seen Lord Ponsonby riding in the park one day and fallen madly—and permanently—in love.

So now there was nothing for her to do except inhale the requisite number of germs and go into a decline. (Although germs of course had not yet been discovered.) She began to be very serious about dying—and nearly did—of scarlet fever. She gradually recovered, but after Ponsonby, Harriette's heart was never really again in her work.

What made another Wilson sick was not love but a British prime minister, Lloyd George. President Woodrow Wilson went to the Paris Peace Conference with high hopes for his League of Nations and perpetual peace. What happened at the conference might have convinced him how visionary his dream was, for his own degree of rage would have inspired killing in a less civilized man. But while his adrenals screamed "moider the bum," the only mayhem allowed a Princeton scholar, a gentleman, and an exponent of peace was against himself. He had a violent heart burn and rabid indigestion, along with neck spasms and furious headaches. He himself attributed it to "bottled up wrath at Lloyd George." At home, Mrs. Wilson and Dr. Grayson managed to keep him soothed by a careful diet and various forms of entertainment. Vaudeville and musical comedy worked particularly well.

The president's sensitive stomach was an old problem for which he dosed himself generously with all manner of powders and home remedies. Since most of them probably contained aspirin, a stomach irritant, they presumably aggravated his unfortunate stomach even more. Finally, he bought a stomach pump and began to use it almost daily.

How Thomas Jefferson would have coped with Lloyd George we do not know, but we do know that while a member of George Washington's cabinet, he and Alexander Hamilton quarreled constantly—and Washington usually sided with Hamilton. This infuriated Jefferson and gave him back and shoulder aches so severe that he resigned and went home to the peace of Monticello. Unfortunately, there he seems to have exchanged a back strained by emotional tension for a genuine physical injury (perhaps a slipped disc) while engaged in the peaceful but dangerous pursuit of farming.

Jefferson was always prone to severe headaches, perhaps migraine, whenever he overworked or was under great pressure. Around 1818 he had an acute attack of rheumatism and blockage of the bowels, believed to have been the result of business worries. Having co-signed a $40,000 bank loan for a friend who defected, Jefferson was forced to mortgage all his own property to make good the loan. A strong gut reaction does not seem unreasonable.

Discussions about plans and designs for the University of Virginia also brought on rheumatism, even though his beautiful and classic designs were adopted. He went to Warm Springs to recover but found the remedy worse than the disease. He decamped in a few days because the company was dull, he had a fever, and had acquired "boils on his seat."

George Washington's illnesses were real enough and dangerous enough but they induced a somewhat unusual attitude toward life. From young manhood, he assumed he was not long for this world and spoke and thought often of his impending demise. The supposed imminence of death seems not to have frightened or particularly depressed him, but made him very pessimistic about every illness except the one that killed him. Of it he proclaimed with optimism, "You know I never have taken anything for a cold; let it go as it came."

By the age of thirty, he had almost died of: "an ague and fever"; smallpox; pleurisy; the bloody flux, dysentery and fever; malarial fever; and pneumonia.

Fortunately for his country, revolutions agreed with him, for during the campaigns, he never seems to have been seriously ill. Once safely in the presidency, however, he had another brush with his old acquaintance, Death, this time blood-poisoning from a large carbuncle on his leg.

Benjamin Franklin invented a bladder catheter thirty years before he developed a need for it himself, and kept right on inventing to the day he died. When Washington visited old Ben on his death bed, Franklin showed Washington his latest invention, a new kind of washing mangle. Franklin had, years before, decided that given the choice between his bladder calculi and doctors, he preferred the stones. He did not consider having them removed although he was "disabled by the stone" just before the Constitutional Convention.

Eventually the calculi gave him extreme pain, but he still said, "My diseases are not very grievous, since I am more afraid of the medicines than the malady."

Daniel Webster's affliction was only seasonal, although he was very grateful for anything a doctor could do—which wasn't much. He had terrible hay fever every year from August 23 to October 1. One August 15 he wrote, "In seven days I shall begin to sneeze and blow my nose." Each summer he left Washington where the pollen count wasn't bad for Marshfield, Massachusetts, where it was. (He almost but never quite caught on to the connection between Marshfield and hay fever.) A famous specialist, Dr. Croes, in New Brunswick, New Jersey, prescribed iodate of iron, hydrodate of potash, and arsenic. In the pollen season of 1851, Webster stayed in Franklin, New Hampshire, while taking his iron, potash, and arsenic and found that Dr. Croes' remedy at least delayed the onset of his misery by about two weeks for which he was truly grateful. (It also happens to be a fact that the ragweed season is two weeks later in Franklin than in Marshfield.) He also tried large amounts of whisky for the hay fever. Since whisky interferes with circulation to the capillaries, the alcohol probably helped nothing except his spirits.

Hay fever, as all true hay fever sufferers know, can be a very serious life problem without antihistamines, and Daniel Webster's interfered with his political and other careers. How it affected his career as a ladies' man, we do not know, but it bothered a fellow lawyer who mentioned the sneezing and blowing as most irritating. At times it kept the fiery orator from speaking engagements, and is believed to be the cause of his resignation from President Fillmore's cabinet.

And the traitorous hay fever of this great American patriot most unpatriotically cleared up in enemy territory. When he visited England in the summer of 1838 his nose behaved with perfect propriety.

A Dr. Morill Wyman finally hit on the diagnosis: "a pollenosis associated with Roman Wormwood [ragweed]." Since by that time Daniel Webster had been dead for twenty years it did him no more good than the conclusion that Scott Fitzgerald had eaten and drunk himself to death, not from a lack of moral fiber, but from a hyper-insulinism which gave him an insatiable craving for sugar, candy, and alcohol. His body, in its blind struggle to keep alive, had killed him.

Marcel Proust, like Immanuel Kant, did not believe in leaving things to the wisdom or the foolishness of the body. He coped very simply with his smallness and frailness. He gave in to it, with such *savoir faire* that his family, his acquaintances, and even the French army went right along with his requirements and took good care of him. He depended openly on the women of his family for money and for help in living. But for his severe asthma problems, Proust had a whole system of wisdom and superstitition to ward off the dread seizures.

His acquaintances grew more or less accustomed to a dinner guest who sat all through the meal almost lost in a large fur-lined overcoat and then took it off before venturing into the cold night air. At a friend's wedding, his clothes were so stuffed with cotton padding that he could hardly squeeze between the pews. In the army (shades of American drill sergeants) he was excused from early morning parade, ditch jumping and anything else he felt to be overtaxing. (He quite enjoyed his army stay.)

A number of American presidents have shared Pepys' "cutting of the stone," although none of them seem to have used it as an alibi for wench-chasing. Before anesthesia the operation was unbearably painful, and when young Jimmy Polk, aged seventeen, had a bladder stone removed, thirty-two years before the first use of ether as an anesthetic, it was a trial by knife to task the courage of a hardened warrior. But the results were worth it, for the stone had stunted his growth as a child and often left him doubled over with pain when he tried to play normally. The operation freed him for an active life.

Although anesthetics would have been available for the cutting of President Chester A. Arthur's gallstones, he escaped the operation altogether because his doctors labeled them "nervous indigestion." But the man Samuel Pepys really would have envied was his spiritual kin, Lyndon Johnson, who had the jolliest gall bladder operation on record. Between the expertise of surgeons at Bethesda, the efficiency of modern painkillers, and the president's own stoutheartedness, he was, in no time, entertaining reporters and cheerfully displaying his wound.

President Kennedy had suffered, but more discreetly, from Addison's disease, or more accurately had had it and *not* suffered, except perhaps from a little widening of the jowls from corticoids, which hurt his pride. This disease, an occasional problem in the Kennedy line, was once very serious indeed but now has been well tamed by cortisones. His wartime back injury, from which he had nearly died, left him in frequent acute pain. The pain was eased somewhat by the Oval Room rocking chair but could be triggered by even such seemingly innocent occasions as a ceremonial tree planting.

Theodore Roosevelt, heartier than Johnson, more stoic than Kennedy, is almost *too* much for us. Nobody should be quite as gung-ho as T.R. Like Kennedy, he had been a sickly child, but much worse. He had several defects attributed by some to inbreeding, the worst of which were poor eyes and violent asthma attacks for which all remedies failed. In desperation his father sent the eleven-year-old Teddy and his sister traveling for four years. This broadened their outlook more than it reduced their illness, although they discovered mountains gave the best relief, and very gradually Teddy began to grow out of his childhood affliction.

Whether from weak bones or foolhardy exuberance, T.R. collected a fine assortment of fractures which seem to have left him totally undaunted. Enemies of fox-hunting will be pleased to learn that these little animals, on Long Island, were his particular nemesis. On one occasion he picked himself up off some rocks with a broken wrist and badly bruised face, got back on his horse, continued riding, and appeared punctually, if much bandaged, for dinner.

While campaigning for the Progressive party in 1912, he bellowed (or would have bellowed except for a high-pitched voice) that he was "fit as a bull moose," a dangerous challenge. The response of an insane hunter was not long in coming. Roosevelt was shot while speaking at a hotel in Milwaukee. Although he staggered from the impact, he felt no pain but prudently checked his lungs by coughing, decided they were intact, and continued speaking, presumably without notes since the speech notes in his breast pocket had stopped the force of the bullet. It is to be doubted whether his audience was able to match his sangfroid and keep its mind on antitrust legislation and off assassins. One is relieved to know that he was exhausted at the end of the speech and willing to go to a hospital, while his listeners presumably restored themselves with Milwaukee's prime product.

Franklin Roosevelt had been a ten-pound baby and grew into a tall handsome young politician, the very picture of the robust American male. Unfortunately, he was generally sickly. He had lumbago. He had stomach pains, apparently appendicitis, for which he was operated upon. And he had chronic nose and throat illnesses, including abscessed tonsils for which he finally had a tonsillectomy at thirty-seven, which he said "was not an agreeable operation." He had been so carefully protected in childhood that public exposure, and exposure to his own children, kept giving him belated childish diseases, topped off, of course, by infantile paralysis for which he had not built up immunity as many children did.

The temperature of the White House has been much like the Three Bears' porridge. Abraham Lincoln found it too cold and drafty and huddled in a gray flannel shawl. Sometimes, even at conferences and cabinet meetings, he sat wrapped like an old grandmother.

President Garfield found the White House much too hot. This attractive, eloquent, popular president (but a little bit of a crook?) was the last president who could legitimately claim to have been born in a log cabin. Garfield had received bullet injuries in the Civil War which resulted in intermittent fevers. The first White House air-conditioning system was designed and built for him.

Air was passed through an iron chamber with three thousand square feet of turkish toweling hung in layers and constantly saturated with ice water. Fans drew the damp air through a second box filled with charcoal to purify it. The air was then blown through a pipe to the president's bedroom, the air pumps being manned presumably by husky, sleepless members of the staff.

Andrew Johnson might just as well have been a crook since he escaped impeachment only by a hair. Self-educated, honest, courageous, and intelligent, the man was so unlucky he couldn't even get a stomachache without ruining his reputation. On the day that Lincoln died, Vice-President Johnson had a gastrointestinal infection. To brace him for his swearing-in as president, the doctor prescribed a shot of whisky. Between the virus and the whisky, Johnson was none too steady on his feet. From that day, his enemies called him a drunkard, although he was known to be exceptionally moderate for a southern gentleman.

But of course nothing like so moderate as Rutherford B. Hayes. He didn't drink and he didn't smoke. Early to bed and early to rise. Eating and exercising sensibly, he enjoyed the best of good health. He even took the power of the presidency so moderately that he never became addicted. He served only one term by his own choice and then retired to a life of quiet good works.

Benjamin Harrison managed to leave the White House in better health than he entered it. He took his responsibilities more lightly than most, apparently content with his place in history as an honest man of very medium abilities.

Perhaps Harrison had not had enough childhood diseases. There have been theories that illness and adversity in childhood foster those qualities of mind and character that lead to greatness. While this theory may be nonsense, lives like Teddy Roosevelt's do seem to stem directly from a struggle to overcome childhood handicaps. On the other hand, his cousin Franklin was an exceptionally healthy child. (His problems came later.) Of course, he had the usual colds and a good many feigned illnesses. Unfortunately, he always gave himself away because he hammed up his suffering. When actually ill, young Franklin took his discomforts with considerable stoicism so as not to upset his parents.

Sickly little John Kennedy's mind was clearly enriched

by the combination of illnesses that often invalided him out of the hyperactive life of the normal Kennedy child and forced him to read and think more.

In the past, many children bore the marks of deficiency diseases. Little—in fact, *very* little—Wolfgang Mozart was a terribly thin, pale child with a big nose inherited from his mother, as well as a bulging forehead and other aftermath of rickets, a disease rarely seen since cod-liver oil. Napoleon was a half-starved kid with acute vitamin deficiencies which probably laid the groundwork for a lifetime of sicknesses.

Children need particular help with flaws that disgrace them in their own eyes and in the eyes of their peers. There are, for example, few more unhappy citizens than small (or worse yet, big) boys who wet the bed. Michael Landon, the well-known television actor, remembers so vividly the shame of this problem, which afflicted him until the age of twelve, that he has prepared a television special on the problem of bed-wetting for the sake of present-day children who suffer the same humiliation. He has also made a point of mentioning it when he guests on talk shows.

Maybe it would have helped young Michael to know that he was at least in the company of kings, and that one royal counterpart had the even greater humiliation of sharing his bed with a sibling who complained at the time and kept on telling the story for the rest of her life. Sleeping with the damp little prince (later to be George III) was an experience his sister, the Duchess of Brunswick, remembered well. "He had been as disagreeable a bedfellow as any royal or plebeian child could be." His Britannic Majesty's uncomfortable juvenile habit was eventually cured

by the insistence of his father—the then Prince of Wales—
that he should wear "a blue ribbon with a china article attached to it," the old lady told Lord Malmesburg.

So the famous have always been like you and me, full
of aches, pains, and foibles. Knowing this is often warmly
companionable, but Mahatma Gandhi on tranquilizers?
Gandhi, the very symbol of peace in a troubled world?
Gandhi, whose picture we have taped to our kitchen
walls, as we sit in lotus position, transcendentally meditat-
ing ourselves into an Eastern calm to face income tax, air
pollution, spouses, violence in the streets, and summer
reruns on television? Gandhi with high blood pressure?
Oh, no.

But there he sat, crosslegged, quietly spinning, in the
midst of the upheaval of his nonviolent revolution, but
inwardly suffering terribly from the strain. And so he
might, this very skimpy David with his dubious slingshot,
against a whole empire. We can surely allow him frailties.
And he had them, partly because of his Spartan life and
increasingly foolish diet which gave him headaches, con-
stipation, and finally dysentery. This, exacerbated by the
region's very hard water, in turn gave him anal fissures
which made him utterly miserable. While convalescing, he
eased his distress by learning to spin and continued to spin
to soothe his nerves. Fortunately, he also had an old Indian remedy for nervous troubles, Rauwolfia serpentine,
derived from a plant, which was finally discovered by
western medicine and began the tranquilizer boom.

If Gandhi's Rauwolfia had only been shared to ease the
frenzy of a fellow vegetarian, Adolf Hitler, the twentieth
century might have taken a sharp turn for the better. If
some magic super-tranquilizer from the future had been

available to dissolve the venom while preserving the genius, Hitler might have achieved his dream of *Deutschland Über Alles*—in music, in scholarship, in invention, in science, or in industrial efficiency, for we glimpse, in the accomplishments of the handful who escaped him, the measure of what Hitler threw away in the throes of his insane torment. Imagine the lives so wastefully and horribly discarded and the lives perverted to his horrifying goals; imagine that talent and energy united under a brilliant charismatic leader toward, not death, but life.

Through the ages, of course, our lives have always hung in the balance of tyrants' disordered physiologies, the gout of kings, or sludge in the arteries of emperors. And we all may go out in a mushroom puff, courtesy of a madman's spleen, or a diplomat's jet-lag stupidity.

Fortunately, medicine has already insured that we won't die from somebody else's gout or even from his syphilis, the combination that transformed a handsome, virile, learned, semi-noble, and wholly pious young English king into the impotent, loathsomely diseased monster, Henry VIII.

On the other hand, would the United States exist at all except for an excruciating disease called porphyria (which cropped up, for some reason, among the descendants of Mary, Queen of Scots)? For porphyria was the scourge that drove King George III mad.

A man who would have loved being an American farmer, maybe a stubborn Vermonter, he went a-farming with his troop of children and forced each (even the most unagrarian) to cultivate a garden plot. George was, in fact, particularly suitable for U.S. citizenship. He even loved baseball. In his childhood it had been his favorite game.

He might have been a good secretary of agriculture, but kingship was certainly neither his talent nor his pleasure. But he *was* a king, maddened (and finally deafened and blinded) by his disease. And the rest is American history.

The Look
of Love

PHYSICAL FLAWS that threaten to deprive one of love are very hard to bear. Especially for the young. Uncertain of their identity, eager to conform, they often accept the cruelest stereotypes unquestioningly. And the stereotypes about love are very cruel. We are told from childhood's first fairy tale to TV's latest commercial that love is for the beautiful and the physically perfect, the exclusive property of the lovely princess and handsome prince (although the tale of the frog prince tries to tell another story). Like most stereotypes, this one has an element of truth. But only an element. Those who take it too seriously do themselves great injustice.

If you're fat and convinced that fat people don't get loved, you very well may not, even though other fat people do. This is known in psychology as a self-fulfilling prophecy. And any psychologist knows that more people fail to win love because they decide they aren't worth loving than ever fail because of physical flaws. A psychotherapist learns a great deal about who loves whom and why (some of it pretty startling), yet as I listen to one of my beautiful patients talking about the man she loves, I slip back into the old fairy tales and, since a pretty girl is worried about losing his love, picture him as conventionally attractive. Then she shows me his picture. I hadn't expected him to be bald, or fat, or undersized (although I've seen some pretty exciting bald, fat, and undersized men myself!). Sophisticated as I may be in the ways of the human heart, when I think of high-class romance I picture a Romeo or Lancelot.

But if you come right down to it, what did Sir Lancelot look like? Since the camera, we can see that royal brides and romantic heroes aren't all that handsome. Perhaps they never were—not even at Camelot! Maybe troubadours found that ballads about a bandy-legged knight and a plump queen named Guinevere (with all that feasting, she probably was) sold better if you prettied them up a bit. And maybe Cinderella wasn't any better-looking than the stepsisters, just more fun to be with on a stuffy occasion (as centuries later, another prince found Wallis Simpson to be, and cheerfully gave up his kingdom for the pleasure of her company). We know Cleopatra was no Elizabeth Taylor because that old gossip Plutarch snitched on her:

For her actual beauty, it is said, was not in itself so remarkable that none could be compared to her, or that none could see her without being struck by it, but the contact of her presence, if you lived with her, was irresistible; the attraction of her person, joining with the charm of her conversation, and the character that attended all she said or did, was something bewitching.

But no matter how philosophical or charming you may be, doesn't there come a time when you must give up on love—when ugliness, or infirmity, or age should make one lay aside all thought and hope of romance, when people must face that they never were, or are not now, suitable for loving? The answer to this lies in history—confusing, surprising, and often encouraging history.

On that memorable morning in Wimpole Street, the world's most improbable Cinderella was thirty-nine years old in an era when a woman ceased to be eligible in her twenties. She was also plain, near-sighted, acutely depressed—and drug-addicted. *And* neurotic—afraid of strangers, changes, almost anything. For six years she had been bedridden and could now no longer stand even with assistance. (Dante Gabriel Rossetti said she had been shut up so long with her spaniel that she looked like one.) That day, in 1845, Elizabeth Barrett, who had never really lived, lay on her couch preparing for death. She knew that her face, grown deathly pallid after long imprisonment and much pain, must soon find its harmonious place against the lining of her coffin. (Victorians, faced so often with illness and bereavement, thought about death that way.)

At sixteen she had fallen from a galloping horse and injured her spine. As the years passed, adding other illnesses, she had reconciled herself more and more to a world of books and imagination; now entering middle age, all thought of the love of man for woman was long past.

If she had had any idea what fate really had in store for her, she would probably have died of shock. If fortune tellers had told her, she would have accused them of making cruel sport of a dying invalid. If she had glimpsed it, she would have thought she was having fevered hallucinations.

That January day, she was to embark on one of history's most famous and certainly one of its happiest romances. Suppose we break the news: Dear Miss B., Quite the nicest, popular, handsome young man in London, your very soulmate, a man so discriminating in his choice of women that he has feared never to find one he could truly love—this young man even now is falling in love with you. Furthermore, he's very dashing and elegant, dark and brilliant, kind, good, everything a woman could desire. Other women, even those reading your story a hundred years from now, will envy you. And this is no tragic romance either. True, you will one day die in his arms, and when you do a biographer will say, "on that day, Robert Browning shut a door in himself and no one ever saw him again, only a splendid surface." With your body in the next room of the Casa Guido, he will write, "How she looks now—how perfectly beautiful." But he will hide his grief for the sake of your child.

Oh, yes, you're going to have a child and boast that "you never saw such a fat, rosy, lively child." That pleasantly pugnacious young man, Robert Browning, will bully you into getting well for love of him. (Your finest poetry, *Sonnets from the Portuguese*, will also be for love of him.)

Next year you will run off, maid, dog and all, to Italy, where you will live together in perfect happiness, you and Robert and, eventually, little Penini. Of course, no man is perfect. There will be that dreadful morning when he shaves off his beard and you burst into tears and are inconsolable until he promises to grow it back immediately. And his totally unreasonable attitude toward your spiritualism, even though all the thinkers are into it! You'll have to write warningly to your sister not to mention it because it brings on "foamings of the mouth in him." And the disgraceful occasion when he threatens to throw the notorious American medium Mr. Home down the stairs. And the time he laughs so hard all through your seance that the spirits are afraid to show up. Otherwise, he's absolutely perfect and you will write that your happiness changes only to increase. But you'd better do something about Flush. That wretched little dog is going to bite your handsome lover—twice.

And that is how it all happened. After that most famous of love letters that began, "I love your verses, dear Miss Barrett" and ended "and I love you too," Robert Browning pursued her relentlessly, at first only by letter, while she replied patiently to his stubborn mind that she was a hopeless invalid, and too old; he would be doing himself an injustice. But as she grew stronger, her protests grew weaker. She let him call (oftener and oftener), but even after his visits began (ninety-one in all) they still wrote to one another, sometimes on subjects too delicate to risk face to face; for these lovers, beneath the Victorian phrasing, communicated frankly enough to satisfy a present-day marriage counselor: about money, about his absurd modesty, and her worry about measuring up to a healthy man's ardent passions. And in their life together they continued to share their deepest feelings and most intimate thoughts, and lived and loved and adored their bright little son.

They had sixteen warm, satisfying, wonderful years together in the Italian sun that all but erased Elizabeth's memory of the physical and emotional imprisonment of Wimpole Street. Even their staid English maid found romance in Italy, and Flush liberated himself into a dog-about-town to return as a triumphant Don Juan (with fleas).

And when the idyll was over, Robert Browning, that frequent skeptic, lived on in absolute certainty that one day he would join her, never to be parted again. In the thirty years that he would have to wait for that reunion, the thought of her was always with him.

Now for a pair of lovers who were so full of physical flaws that they were, as one lady put it, "the ugliest couple I have ever seen." He was undersized and frail, in perennial ill health, and smallpox-scarred. His quick, nervous movements, his grimacing and gesticulating, reminded observers of an animated monkey, or, worse yet, a foreigner.

He was also amusing, gay, lively, a little vulgar, utterly charming, as well as kind, generous—and sexy. His handshake, said one lady, was an invitation to the divorce court. Few could resist him, for he had an everlasting current of youth; it was impossible to be dull in his company. His name was George Henry Lewes, "a prince of journalists."

She, on the other hand, was shy and ill at ease, with an awkward, dumpy figure, gauche manner, and heavy, ill-matched features. She had been mistaken for a middle-aged woman while still in her teens. Her head was so massive that it fascinated phrenologists; her total appearance was the despair of matchmaking friends. She had no clothes sense, and left to herself was hopelessly dowdy. Even when older and better groomed, she struck people as funny-looking, her big face framed in Parisian creations, frequently topped with an immense ostrich plume.

That's how her *friends* described her. A jealous rival put it less graciously: "Badly dressed, essentially underbred and provincial, holding her hands and arms kangaroo fashion," and having in her chosen clothes, "an unwashed, unbrushed, unkempt look altogether."

Indeed, George Eliot's horsey face in high school and college textbooks has been an inspiration to countless adolescent females uncertain of their beauty and allure, for if that was the face of a sex symbol, capable of inspiring scandalous romance, we could all hope that, in good time, we too would emerge as femmes fatales. Of course, she had a transfiguring smile and a vibrant, amorous voice, so we might have to spend some time practicing our ravishing smiles and throatiness. But there was, at least, hope.

With her lovingness and sympathetic manner, and by the fascination of her shared thoughts, she drew men and women toward her. After an hour's talk a stranger came away so bemused he thought her beautiful. Another who fell in love with her found her the most fascinating creature he had ever seen. Charles Bray, a lifelong and happily married friend said: "The most delightful companion I have ever known; she knew everything . . . her aim was always to show her friends off to advantage, not herself."

Perhaps her greatest asset was that George Eliot genuinely liked men—of all ages, as it turned out. When she was twenty-four, a friend of sixty-two enjoyed talking and walking with her so much that his wife threatened to leave him if the young woman didn't leave first. When she was in her thirties, a boy of twenty was so captivated by a few meetings that while he never saw her again, as an old man he noted in his diary the anniversary both of his birth and her death. Even the handsome philosopher Herbert Spencer, who lived long and loved no one, enjoyed her camaraderie and was so impressed by her transfixing smile and vibrant voice that he almost forgot himself.

George Henry Lewes, who had lived in a commune and more than half believed in free love, took one long look and forgot not only himself but everyone else. He adored her and her alone until the day he died. And feminists ever since have adored *him*, for he not only loved his Polly, he did for her what countless women but few men have ever done for their talented mates. He devoted his life to her happiness and success, often at the expense of his own literary career. He knew that while his work was good, hers was potentially great, and he wanted the whole world to see her genius and know her as he did.

He was everything to her—loving mate, court jester when her too-serious nature needed lightening, literary agent, public relations man, delightful host who surrounded her with the literary world of her day and gave her social ease. He told her firmly that she was capable of writing novels and made her try, at first perhaps only to please him. He was, in fact, as necessary to the creation of her books as a sperm is necessary to the creation of a human life.

Together they also created one of the juicier Victorian scandals. For he was, indeed, everything to her but one. He was not her husband, having a thoroughly legal if also thoroughly unfaithful wife. When the dowdy thirty-two-year-old spinster Mary Anne Evans decamped to the Continent with a lawfully wed father of three, London and her family were appalled. And when they returned and set up housekeeping, the social disgrace was complete. In fact, she used a pen name partly because a scarlet woman's book would not be welcome on the table of a respectable household.

Since she could not carry Lewes' last name, she chose his first one and became George Eliot, whose *Silas Marner* never once tempted us young to even the smallest sin although he was, as I recall it, better than *Robinson Crusoe* or a summer vacation with Thackeray's *Henry Esmond*.

So for twenty-three years George Eliot made a loving home for George Lewes and his three grateful sons, who adored her and were happy to call her "Mutter." And gradually a liaison which had shocked, came to be accepted for what it was: a stable, respectable household and a warm gathering place for many distinguished friends (Richard Wagner and Ralph Waldo Emerson on the same afternoon) until Lewes died. And then George Eliot did it again!

She got married. At sixty-one. To a man twenty-one years younger, but just as devoted as the last. She married with the blessing of Lewes's son who believed, with reason, that his father would have wanted whatever made her happy.

Revived from her mourning by the new relationship, George Eliot had a renaissance; even her health seemed better. "Marriage," she wrote, "has seemed to restore me to my old self. I seem to have recovered the loving sympathy I was in danger of losing."

In their happy months together, she and her husband went traveling and sightseeing, and spent many hours reading to one another, he listening with the old enchantment to the "rich, deep, organlike tones" that had always attracted men. And when she died on December 22, 1880, the cemetery, even in bitter sleet and snow, was crowded by the men and women who had adored her.

Lord Acton wrote: "It seems to me as if the sun had gone out. You cannot think how I loved that woman." Henry James thought her mind one of the most beautiful on earth. Her stepson could never speak of her without tears. Even Eliza Lynn, the cattiest of her critics (who had once compared her to a kangaroo), said, "She was loved by all men and passionately regarded by many. She might have changed her partner when she would during Mr. Lewes' lifetime, and after his death, if she had not married Mr. Cross, she might have married others."

In other words, George Eliot was one very attractive and sexy dame. Marilyn Monroe would have given her soul for one-tenth the love and care that enveloped George Eliot, and even more if she could have received the kind of loving care that George Eliot herself gave to the men and women who surrounded her.

Dolley Madison was a woman so unlike George Eliot that she herself has no place in this book. She shared with George Eliot only two things: a weakness for ostrich plumes and the affection of everyone who knew her. Her husband, "Jemmy" Madison, fourth president of the United States, chief framer of the Constitution, and broadest scholar among the Founding Fathers, had plenty of flaws. His physique was unfortunate. Smallest of all American presidents, he was so frail and puny that he rarely weighed a hundred pounds, and so wizened that somebody said of this ex-theological student, "He had the high, bald forehead and the worried look of a premature infant born into a world for which it is not ready." Socially he was "slow, unimpassioned, and unmagnetic." By the time Aaron Burr brought him to call on young widow Todd, he had been jilted at least twice.

The effect of Dolley upon this austere, sexless-seeming man was galvanic. Forsaking his usual shyness with all speed, he proposed. Dolley had looked forward to meeting "the great little Madison" and found she liked him but did not begin by falling in love with her plain, awkward, forty-three-year-old suitor. The marriage was probably, for her, one of convenience. The twenty-four-year-old Dolley had come through a rough time. A few months earlier she had watched her husband and infant son die in a virulent epidemic, barely surviving herself. She had a small child to support and a mother who needed help. Mr. Madison's plantation would provide a secure and gracious living. That was enough.

But she grew to feel differently about James Madison. She may have looked down on him physically (she was a head taller and a good many pounds heavier), but she certainly looked up to him as a man to love, honor, and respect. They seem to have been one of the happiest of presidential couples, and the White House has never been a livelier, happier, and more hospitable place. It has been said of her: "She loved parties and she loved shops; she loved people and she loved things; she loved her husband and she loved her home; and into the world she spilled sunshine which still sparkles along the way she went."

She charmed even that elegant, hard-to-please man-about-town, Washington Irving. Lafayette, who had visited all the courts of Europe, could find no duchess, no princess to equal her. "She moves like a goddess and she looks like a queen," he said; her manner, "with equal dignity blended equal sweetness." She had a good time just being alive but was always careful to enhance her husband's popularity and prestige and lived always within the security of their love for one another. Unlike George Eliot's situation, here it was the woman who gave the man an ease and social popularity that his seeming austerity could not encompass. In both cases, the mates were worthy of the love given and received.

Unlike the Brownings and George Eliot, the Madisons

leave behind no love poetry, no passionate diaries, no novels, and very few letters of any kind that spell out the depth and quality of their feeling for one another.

As for passion between husband and wife, the early Americans rarely give us a clue except by the frequent emergence of little early Americans. The Madisons do not give us even that hint. Reports of early presidents shield us from knowledge of their humanness or even of their humor. After many pages, one is astonished to discover that Madison could be funny, even during his last illness. When told not to struggle to talk while lying down, he quipped, "Oh! I always talk more easily when I lie."

We do not know how undersized young Jemmy Madison had felt when jilted by young ladies. He was not the type to throw himself on the floor in howling tantrums as his contemporary, the Prince Regent of England, was wont to do whenever *he* was crossed in love.

Nor do we know Madison's feelings that September day in Virginia when Dorothea Todd became his wife. We do know that all his life he spoke of it as the most fortunate day of his life—and he was quite right. We know that every visible aspect of their marriage was comfortable and pleasant. We know her name was in his thoughts because it crept into his state letters, and statesmen remembered to please him by asking for Dolley in their replies.

She fussed over him, and her pampering was as good for her husband as it was bad for her scapegrace son. She was so frantic for the president's safety during the sacking of Washington by the British, that after she had reached safety she made the terrified coachman turn back in the hope of finding her husband and rescuing him.

The intellectual abyss between his scholarship and her

avoidance of any heavy mental effort never seems to have prevented them from enjoying one another's company. (A few people, noticing that Dolley was absolutely brilliant in knowing what not to say, suspected her of having more brains than she flaunted.)

When James Madison and his wife retired to his plantation in Virginia, their "cheery companionship" continued and deepened. They had always been gracious and helpful to one another's families, and now, at Montpelier, she was a very loving daughter to his mother, still, at ninety, as intellectual as ever. He was a generous, far too generous, father to her profligate son.

As Madison grew older, Dolley scarcely permitted him out of her sight and care. While away at the University of Virginia, of which he was a governor, he had been taken ill, and Dolley had been frantic until word arrived that he was better. A letter vividly describes her relief—how she had packed her "cloaths" and kept a carriage ready to fly to him at a moment's notice. "How bitterly I regret not going with you," she wrote. "If business sh'd detain you longer—or you sh'd feel unwell again, let me come for you. . . . My mind is so anxiously occupied about you that I cannot write. May angels guard thee, my dear best friend."

Physically unappealing Jemmy Madison had done extremely well for himself in the sweepstakes of love. They were nice people together, these two. And either an unsuspected physical toughness in this most sickly-looking of presidents, or Dolley's love and care and the enjoyment of her company (friends thought it was Dolley), kept him alive longer than any other man who ever served two grueling terms in the office of president (until wiry little

Harry Truman came along and outdid him by six months).

The flawed appearance of Richard Burton, famous nineteenth-century explorer and adventurer, was very different from that of Dolley's quiet gentleman from Virginia. No helpless infant, he of the "sullen eyes of a stinging serpent." If Jemmy Madison gave one the impression he needed sheltering from the world, Richard Burton looked as if the world might need protection from him. He had, wrote a British consul who encountered him in Buenos Aires, "a countenance the most sinister I have ever seen, dark, cruel, treacherous, with eyes like a wild beast's. He reminded me by turns of a black leopard, caged but unforgiving. . . . He wore habitually a rusty black coat with a rumpled black silk stock, his throat destitute of collar, a costume which his muscular frame and immense chest made singularly hideous." He also "grew dangerous in his cups and drank too much." The consul might have added, as somebody else did, that Burton knew thirty-five languages and dialects, particularly the language of pornography.

The reaction of a gently reared, nineteen-year-old daughter of the Catholic aristocracy of England, when she glimpsed Richard Burton on the ramparts of Boulogne, was somewhat different. "That man," she announced to her sister when she had recovered sufficiently from the shock of his appearance to be capable of speech, "will marry me," and went home to prepare herself for this high calling. She soon learned enough about him to realize that extensive preparation would be desirable.

Richard, chronologically ten years and in experience a hundred years older than Isabel, had been everywhere, and, people suspected, had done everything—and had been indiscreet enough to write about a lot of it.

As a soldier in India disguised by native costume he had spied on the natives. At the casual suggestion of a senior officer, he had reported on sexual perversions in the province so thoroughly that the London Foreign Office never recovered from its shock and suspicion of Richard. He compiled a monkey dictionary; learned snake charming; experimented with opium; and took up yoga, hypnosis, and the occult. He held a diploma as a master dervish. In his talk "he affected an extreme brutality, and if one could have believed the whole of what he said, he had indulged in every vice and committed every crime." He rather approved of cannibalism. He was no fit husband for a nice English girl.

As Isabel's parents immediately perceived. Isabel was shocked, in turn, by their and the world's blindness to the genius and virtue of her intended. She set herself to enlightening them, a crusade she was to continue as maid, wife, and widow for the rest of her life. "If I were a man," she wrote to her understandably difficult mother, "I would be Richard Burton; but, being only a woman, I would be Richard Burton's wife. . . . I have *got* to be with him day and night for *all my life.*" Otherwise, she threatened, she would become a sister of charity.

Fortunately, this proved unnecessary. She got him— but only after ten years of waiting, watching, and praying (she never doubted that God, having greater wisdom than her parents, would be on her side). They were ten years in which the elusive Richard went to the holy city of Mecca (forbidden to infidels on pain of death); rejoined his Indian regiment long enough to generate the usual warm dislike; made an expedition to the even more dangerous city of

Harar in Somaliland; fought all through the Crimean War,
but as usual only with his superiors; came home (Isabel
caught him long enough this time to get engaged); took off
for Africa for another three years in search of the source of
the Nile and, being Richard Burton, just missed it; and returned looking even worse than before. Isabel refusing to
elope (she later agreed), he departed on another religious
pilgrimage, this time to Salt Lake City, where the Mormons stuffily refused him as a convert. Loving initiation
rites, he customarily joined whatever religious sect he happened to be studying. Finding the Mormons' sexual mores
disappointingly dull after Arabia, he returned without a
plurality of wives, to Isabel's intense relief. She was taking
no more chances, and setting herself "XVIII Rules of
Wifehood," including under the circumstances the very
wise command "not to make prudish bothers," she picked
the first date astrologically auspicious for both of them
and, at nearly thirty, she became Richard Burton's wife.

Mission accomplished, she set her sights again. She
must win him to Roman Catholicism, otherwise how
could she be sure of keeping her beloved through all eternity. And he must be *Sir* Richard Burton. This uphill task
took twenty-seven years of politicking and recovering his
good name as fast as he could bury it, while the two of
them racketted around the world to minor diplomatic
posts—São Paulo, Teneriffe, Trieste, Damascus—where
he invariably stirred up new furors and she invariably
sympathized and redoubled her polishing of his damaged
halo.

At Damascus he outdid himself, uniting Moslems,
missionaries, Greeks, Jews, and English residents in a single purpose—to get rid of Richard.

As for Richard and Isabel Burton and their marriage,

they had a marvelous time together. Ouida, an outrageous lady author of lurid romances, who also fancied Richard, thought him, "sardonic, caustic, stern" and said that he "looked like Othello and lived like the Three Musketeers." She complained that "he had one unpardonable fault, he loved his wife . . . his love for her was extreme . . . a love marriage in the absolute sense of the word, not wise on either side, but on each impassioned."

When it was all over, Isabel said Richard had not only been the best husband in the world but the pleasantest and easiest man to live with. Ouida might have found him disappointingly tame! Even Richard had to admit that he had never actually killed another man.

And at seventy, busier than ever with his *Scented Garden* and other Eastern erotica, and as dangerous-looking as possible, Richard could be found relaxing with a copy of *Little Lord Fauntleroy* and playing with his pet kitten. (When he died, it didn't want to leave him.) Maybe the caged leopard had never been quite as black and deadly as it pretended.

Isabel, the widow, chatted with Richard's spirit daily and settled down to write an immense *Life* "Consecrated to My Earthly Master Who Is Waiting For Me On Heaven's Frontiers." Getting him ensconced in that proper Christian paradise had been even more uphill than his ascent into the British peerage. Isabel achieved it, but only by taking his salvation firmly, as usual, into her own two capable hands. Once, in Brazil, she baptized him herself (to such good effect that he promptly recovered). When he finally did die, she refused to admit it had happened until the priest arrived; and if by any bureaucratic error she failed to find Richard at the pearly gates, she would merely have started campaigning until the oversight was corrected.

Since their life together on earth had been full of comradeship, adventure, and laughter, perhaps an eternity of Isabel's company made up for the lost happy hunting grounds and beautiful dancing girls of Richard's other projected paradises.

The storm she stirred up with his Episcopalian relatives by snatching him into a Roman Catholic heaven was nothing compared to the funeral pyre she made of his manuscripts to sanctify his earthly status. Scholars, anthropologists, and pornographers are never likely to forgive her for that holocaust.

For, with all his bombast, bigotry, and lunacy, and his virtually unreadable mishmashes (never has the prurient mind had to work so hard for its titillation) of geography, lyric scenery, mind-boggling statistics, religious observations, sexual mores, and loathsome diseases (particularly of the genitalia), Sir Richard Francis Burton still rates a whole page of fine print in the *Encyclopaedia Britannica* (Isabel would be furious with the editors for giving him only one page). He was a valuable explorer, a very accurate observer, an extensive anthropologist, and the first of the scientific writers on sexual subjects, from Krafft-Ebing and Havelock Ellis to Margaret Mead and Alfred Kinsey and on at last to Masters and Johnson. He would have been right at home in the Elizabethan era or, better yet, our own, with our enjoyment of exotic TV personalities and our passion for pornography. We'd have given him enough recognition to please even his wife—or almost.

So far we have proved that if one merits love, one may achieve it no matter how bad one looks. A far less noble verity now appears, for that worthless cad, Gabriele D'Annunzio, was even more ugly on the inside than on the outside. The beloved of Eleanora Duse (and a number of other high-class ladies who should also have had their heads examined) was not prepossessing in any way to the uninfatuated.

He had a small face with sunken cheeks, deep smallpox pits, a big nose, bulging eyes, and, by the time he was twenty-five, a bald head. He was also a snob, a liar, a double-crosser, a thief, and, eventually, the spiritual father of Italian fascism. He also had bad teeth and foul breath.

But he wrote magnificently explicit pornographic novels. (The first, written at seventeen, transformed the two kindly spinsters of his kindergarten years into a pair of elderly sex maniacs.) He also wrote poetry which would have been good if it were less ornate, and he had an eloquent hard sell that captured the beautiful and aristocratic ladies already excited by the promise of his erotica.

His dress was splendiferous. For a small holiday in Egypt with Duse, he gave the list of his wardrobe to the press. Among other items, he was packing:

    72 shirts
    48 drawers (with lace and other embellishments)
    14 dozen socks
    72 pairs of gloves
    18 umbrellas and parasols
    150 neckties
    16 pairs of shoes (2 for hunting crocodiles)

and to be on the safe side: 1 carbine, 3 revolvers, and 1 dagger and, of course, innumerable hats and sundries including "one dainty and elegant lap dog."

Eleanora Duse, foremost actress of her day, was a lovely, gentle woman, renowned for the naturalness and simplicity of her stage portrayals. The critics of the day, including George Bernard Shaw, waxed lyrical over Duse. One described her as "a chalice for the wine of the imagination." And this sensitive, reserved woman went completely ape over D'Annunzio.

When she carried on like a school girl, and she did, over a man so patently unworthy of her (that is, patent to everybody but Eleanora), the distress of her admirers was great. When he cast her aside, they affixed the word *Cad* to his name as firmly as if his parents had given it to him. Anyhow, Duse made a terrible fool of herself, as only a loving woman can. Much to the annoyance of the mistress *in situ,* she sent him twelve telegrams for his birthday, one to be delivered each hour. Once, while driving, she caught a bee in her bare hands and endured its furious sting lest it hurt her beloved Gabriele.

He repaid her by writing a much acclaimed (at the time) erotic novel about an elderly actress (sagging chin, crepelike throat, crow's-feet, dark rings) and a young handsome writer (D'Annunzio was five years her junior) with a fine head of hair. The sex scenes were as explicitly described as a 1970s sex manual, and the book made him, for the first time, internationally famous—and rich.

Duse, the most patient Griselda since Chaucer's original, besottedly gave up Ibsen and Shakespeare to wage a campaign on behalf of D'Annunzio's lifeless plays. Driven to her greatest heights to make her lover's dramas come alive, she made not them but herself immortal—the Immortal Duse (the plays collect dust and antiquarians in obscure library corners).

Never for a moment would D'Annunzio have believed

their fate as he wrote his intended masterpieces, the Duse adoringly at his feet. He took up horseback riding in preparation for the equestrian statues that would be raised to his fame.

Presently it was time for new women. First a peasant (because he liked her perspiration) who shortly had to be committed to an asylum; then a lady of pedigree who eventually turned from sin to a mountain convent, became a mother superior and in a 1923 blizzard set out to visit a hospice for travelers and was found frozen to death in the snow. Before this chilling denouement, one is gratified to know that the lady, and her furious husband, gave our hero a hard time; she never made it clear, as she brandished her pistols in an overwrought condition, whether the projected death was marked His or Hers.

Long afterward, Eleanora Duse developed a sense of humor about D'Annunzio (the description of her last visit to the aging ex-enchanter is quite funny). But now, going into middle age, she took his defection very hard. It did her career a world of good, however. Once rid of the blight of his stodgy plays, she soared, her dramatic power deepened by the suffering she had endured.

Meanwhile, without Duse's profitable partnership to make money for him, and with no inclination to curb the splendor of his purchases, D'Annunzio was soon forced to hide out in France under a series of assumed names. He lived there ignobly until World War I gave him an opportunity for patriotism, derring-do, and oratory, which led to the birth of fascism, the loss of an eye, and the enhancement of his already overinflated ego. He furnished himself a special room suitable for the death of a hero and rehearsed the event, although he also fancied being dumped from Auguste Piccard's stratospheric balloon.

He provided himself with a villa by the simple act of moving in and stealing it and its furnishing, including a Rembrandt, from a poor German widow. When she called upon him in an understandably disturbed frame of mind, he gave her a drink which made her sick for weeks. She thought it had probably been a love potion to still her protest. Mussolini conferred a title on him, the Prince of Monteneoso, and D'Annunzio was well settled. But perhaps his thirty-five watchdogs were a good idea.

After the war Duse lived in poverty and illness, until at the age of sixty-six she made a comeback with a triumphal tour of Europe and finally America, where she died (in Pittsburgh, of a cold, on Easter Monday, 1924).

The services in Naples were attended by the envoys of all nations and D'Annunzio had to scramble for the limelight to outdo Mussolini in showing his devotion. Gabriele himself died, at seventy-four, too quickly to be able to stage a proper scene in his dying room, and without any heroic embellishments except the flowery hero's epitaph which he himself had composed

And now to a nicer story about another small man who unlike D'Annunzio has made millions of people happy, a fairy tale about, as a fairy tale should be, a poor boy who grew up to win the love of a princess.

Once upon a time, in the village of Temun in Siberia there lived a humble Jewish cantor and his eight children, the youngest of whom was called Israel. When Israel was four years old, Cossacks swept down upon the little town in a terrible pogrom, burning houses and injuring and killing townspeople, while Israel, his parents, and his seven brothers and sisters huddled in terror in a field outside the town.

The father knew that he must leave the little town

and find safety for his family in the strange new land of America. They settled in a place called the Lower East Side, which the old man and his wife sometimes thought more dangerous than the land of the Cossacks, especially for their youngest son who was not developing into a leader of his people as his parents hoped, but into a tough slum kid; not steeped in the wisdom of the Torah but in the lore of the street gangs; not singing the haunting chants of the synagogue, although his voice promised to be as fine as his father's, but shouting out "Ta-ra-ra-boom-de-ay." Was that any song for a nice Jewish boy, the son of a cantor yet? The parents knew their youngest son would come to some bad end swimming in the East River at the foot of Cherry Street. After his father died, exhausted by this alien new world, Israel's mother's worries intensified, for, mesmerized by the glorious lights and exciting music of the saloons along the Bowery, the boy longed to be part of this glamorous world. Such shame a mother should have—my son the singing waiter? So Israel ran away from home and almost immediately prospered. The very next day he earned twenty-five cents guiding a blind singer from bar to bar. Soon he was making fifty cents some days, almost a wealthy man. When he was fourteen, a saloon keeper pretended not to notice his age and there he was, a singing waiter and as serious-minded and ambitious a young fellow as any parent could want. One night a real prince (Louis of Battenburg, grandfather of the present Duke of Edinburgh) came to the saloon, liked our hero's singing and offered him a tip. The next day a newspaper came out with a long sentimental story (by a young reporter also headed for fame, Henry Bayard Swope) about a mere singing waiter who had turned down a princely tip ($5) with a lordly wave of his democratic hand.

A rival café had a songwriter who had actually had a song published. Israel's boss was not to be outdone. *His* waiters would write a song. Our hero was selected to write the lyrics. It netted him thirty-seven cents in royalties, a new name, and the wonder of seeing it right there on a sheet of music— "Marie from Sunny Italy," and under the picture of a gondola: Words by I. Berlin.

So onward and upward, literally, since the entertainment world meant uptown. No longer the Bowery but Union Square, not quite the center of fashionable entertainment anymore but it still had the Hippodrome and Tony Pastor's. And Luchow's still attracted celebrities of the theater. But, alas, our hero's success was short-lived. He fell asleep while his employer's cash register was being robbed.

In the meantime, far, far away in the kingdom of Long Island, there lived in his palatial residence a very rich and aristocratic czar of capitalism with a beautiful daughter named Ellin. Now Ellin was as charming as she was beautiful, as good as she was charming, as talented as she was good, and, as events were to show, as wise as she was talented. No imposter with poisoned apples could fool the Princess Ellin. *She* would never lose her slipper like that flibbertigibbet Cinderella. No, the Princess Ellin was a very smart 1920s cookie with all her marbles. Which was too bad for her father, the czar, since Clarence Mackay was very, very fond of his beautiful princess and determined she would wed none but the most eligible young man in all Christendom. One is not, after all, the heiress to $20 million with a second-generation listing in the social register for nothing.

So he gave royal balls and invited the most noble and heroic knights of the period. On one memorable night, the grounds of the palace glowed with the light of a thousand lanterns and the trees twinkled with many thousand more tiny lights. The great hall with its ancient tapestries and feudal armor had never looked more magnificent, for it was to honor the heir to the throne of the greatest empire of the world. As Ellin danced with the handsome, golden prince, her father's heart must have glowed with pride.

Their conversation would have jarred him considerably. The Prince of Wales was, or so the legend goes, substituting for Dear Abby and listening sympathetically to a woeful tale of father-crossed lovers. And he kept Papa engaged long enough for Ellin to slip away and telephone her own true love, the mere thought of whom transformed her father into an ogre of the worst fee-fie-fo-fum variety.

His mad daughter had fallen hopelessly in love with an undernourished-looking writer of Tin Pan Alley music, of course by now fabulously rich and successful, but, still, a social nobody and definitely not a proper Catholic. Moses Baline, the only other human being who could have fully appreciated the enormity of the situation, was dead and could make no protest except to turn over in his grave at the thought of a son who might have been a perfectly respectable cantor in a synagogue, but had instead written frivolous music, and now had taken up with a shiksa.

Ellin did her best. She explained how wonderful her songwriter was. After all, had not Irving Berlin written a show for the Army, dozens of beautiful songs, and five Broadway shows? (There were eventually to be forty-seven movies and shows, and well over three thousand songs. Half the popular songs stored in the backs of our minds, composer unknown, turn out to be by Irving Berlin—songs from "Easter Parade" to "It's a Lovely Day Tomorrow.") But Clarence Mackay was not a man to be impressed by "Oh, How I Hate to Get Up in the Morning," "Alexander's Ragtime Band," or the Ziegfeld Follies. He hired private detectives in the firm belief that a man who wrote that kind of music must have a shady past, or, better yet, a shady present. He also threatened to disinherit, hoping money would talk, especially when it came in multimillions.

But Berlin opened fire with heavier artillery. He wrote her love songs. And on January 4, 1926, he carried her off to City Hall (by subway, the first Ellin had ever seen) in such haste that he forgot his wallet. This impasse resolved, they were married. Her father continued his ogreish stance for several years, but eventually softened, and even found he liked his brash son-in-law *and* his dark-eyed little granddaughters. And everybody lived happily ever after, just as in the love songs Irving Berlin wrote for his princess.

The Eye
of the Beholder
and the Shape
of Romance

*H*ow do you look? That depends on who is doing
the looking, for there's no way you can be that you won't
be unattractive to somebody and attractive to somebody
else. And not only do your looks depend on who is looking at you but also when. First meetings can be exceptionally unrewarding, admiration-wise.

When the poet John Keats, that connoisseur of
beauty, met seventeen-year-old Miss Fanny Brawne, he
catalogued her charms and lack thereof in total prose. She
had, he wrote, "a countenance of the lengthened sort: she
wants sentiment in every feature" (surely a fatal flaw to
this poet). "Her nostrils are fine though a little painful," he

continued, "her mouth is good and bad; her profile better than her full face, which indeed is not full but pale and thin." He found her hands "baddish," her feet "tolerable," and her deportment awful.

But very soon all Keats knew and all he needed to know was that he loved Fanny Brawne with a terrible aching passion. Which changed her appearance entirely! He raved about her beauty in such superlatives that she began to complain that he loved her for her beauty alone, whereupon the poor man had to reverse himself again and assure her that her beauty was as nothing to him compared to her sterling qualities of mind and heart. Whether or not her beauty was apparent to his acquaintances, her sterling qualities weren't. To them she was a cold-hearted five-letter word wanting, as Keats originally observed, sentiment in every feature. His friends came to hate her as they watched their poet slipping away from life, longing in vain for letters from his beloved.

Louis XIV said of his brother's wife, Princess Henrietta of England, that she reminded him of the bones in the Cemetery of the Innocents. Although the lady was pretty, she had a hunched back and a consumptive cough. She was too tall and, as Louis complained, far too thin and bony. This complaint can be filed under famous last words. Louis began to be totally fascinated by her and she became one of the most rewarding and versatile of royal mistresses. His brother, having been deliberately raised by their mother to be homosexual, did not miss her. (She died suddenly, perhaps poisoned by one of his lovers.) She was a warm, vivacious, pleasure-loving and good woman, but what pleased everyone was her pleasure in pleasing others. (Molière described her as always smiling.) She even had a warm and affectionate relationship with her brothers Charles II and James II of England, startling for royal siblings.

So if somebody, at first meeting, thinks you look like a bag of bones, think nothing of it. (Alexandre Dumas described young Sarah Bernhardt as having the face of a virgin and the body of a broomstick.)

Louis' objection was unusual. While he was enormously vain and distressed by his small size and baldness, he was very tolerant of flaws in his mistresses. His first instructor in love, supplied in the European tradition that a boy's first partner should be well recommended and experienced in the art of love, was the Comtesse de Beauvais, fat and middle-aged, and with only one eye, but, as the account puts it, "of an ardent temperament." And with her, the fourteen-year-old king discovered he liked the pastime of sex very much. His boyhood love (some said his only real love) was that homely girl, Marie Mancini. In a family of court beauties, Marie was a very ugly duckling. Even her father, the astrologer, foresaw no romantic future for this child. The only sensible thing seemed to be to make her into a nun and get her out of sight as fast as possible. Marrying her off would be just too difficult. But her uncle was Cardinal Mazarin, and she might as well have a time at court, just in case.

Young Louis, not yet eighteen, might be a mighty monarch but he too had been a neglected, unhappy child. As he grew to know Marie, he discovered, in the words of Alexandre Dumas, that "if nature had somewhat neglected her face, it had richly endowed her mind." She was charming, she chattered delightfully, and she clearly loved him "with all the qualities of her heart and mind." The King fell madly in love with her, "as amorous of her mind as of her person."

The young lovers had a pitifully short time together before Louis was forced to marry a Spanish princess as part of a treaty with Spain, and Marie was married off well but unwillingly to a middle-aged public official.

Louise de Vallière, the saddest of Louis' mistresses, had crippled feet and was lame. She was sad, however, not because of her feet, but because she was one of those women who seem determined to evoke bad treatment from men. She was also a very boring (if good) lady who kept demanding that Louis send her to an austere convent. At thirty-one, she succeeded, did penance, got fat, and found peace.

Madame de Maintenon was not one of Louis' mistresses, although she is often listed among them. She held on to her virtue until the queen died and they could be married, albeit secretly. She was older than Louis and was fifty by the time they married, yet the older woman kept his affection for thirty years, when the youngest and most beautiful of his mistresses had not been able to hold him. She was exactly what the overly serious Louis needed. At sixty, despite rheumatic aches and pains, she danced and rode to the hunt with him. At seventy, teeth gone, sight and hearing beginning to go, she went "frolicking piously" in the king's gondolas. At eighty, she accompanied him as the old king drove his coach and six madly along the roads of Versailles. And she held on to her sense of the absurdity of life to the end. (She was wise and clever and had written some of the wittiest epigrams in French literature.) When Peter the Great of Russia visited her on her deathbed and asked, "Of what are you dying, Madame?" she replied, "Of laughter, of laughter."

On the whole Louis was impervious to the blind eye, hunched shoulders, lame legs, and aged wrinkles, if not quite to skinniness, in mistresses. Elizabeth I of England, on the other hand, could not bear the sight of disability or disfigurement in herself or anyone else, and would rarely even give an audience to anyone with an obvious physical impairment.

Then there's the story of Frederick the Great and the two princesses. Frederick generally was not attracted to any women (Frederick fitted the Freudian theory of homosexuality to perfection, with his maniacally brutal father and selfish, over-indulgent mother). His mother was eager for a marriage between her son and her English niece, Princess Amelia, to give her more political leverage. Young Frederick grew up mooning over his cousin (whom he had never seen) and her beauty, and was furious when his father betrothed him instead to a German princess. He hated the interloper (again sight unseen) and described her as "that hideous creature." An unprejudiced observer might have seen little to choose from between the two princesses.

Not only are you at the mercy of other people's prejudices, but even if they like your looks today, there's no guarantee they will tomorrow. Lord Byron announced,

> There be none of Beauty's daughters
> With a magic like thee;
> And like moonlight on the waters
> Is thy sweet voice to me:

and three weeks later described the lady as a damned bitch. And the sheik of Araby who wrote in a sonnet,

> My mistress' eyes are nothing . . .
> If hairs be wires, black wires grow upon her head . . .

seems to have been in a nasty frame of mind, requiring all of a Scheherazade's soothing tricks to bring him round.

Alexander Pope, remembered for good poetry and bad humor, has received much pity for his stunted growth and twisted back which caused noble ladies to scorn him most cruelly. At least, they said some awful things to and about him. But what he said about them! Of course, he attributed their venom to his physical infirmity, and is so convincing in his bitterness that one forgets that a woman also died for love of Alexander Pope. When he was young, he and a beautiful girl were very much in love and wished to marry. When obstacles separated them, she could not bear the thought of life without him and committed suicide.

Yet if one has a physical flaw, it's helpful to be a king or a president. Your flaws may even become the fashion. When a king of Spain lisped, so did the Spanish nobility, which is why today when you speak Castilian, you must do it with an elegant lisp and say Barthelona and not Barcelona.

Because Edward VII's beautiful Danish wife was lame, the fashionable ladies of Edwardian England cultivated the "Alexandra limp." And when President John Kennedy arrived at the White House with his backache and rocking chair, chairs began to rock all over the nation.

Some people (and nations) regard their own looks as the only proper ones, and in their chauvinism, consider all others seriously flawed. Here, for example, is a list of a few terrible flaws: blond hair, black hair, white skin, dark skin, brown eyes, green eyes, round eyes, and slanty eyes. Each of these has been enough to make other groups of people find you repulsive. For a long time, Orientals seemed unattractive to Occidentals, but nothing like so awful as Caucasians looked to the Orientals.

When the United States forced Japan to trade with the

West at gunpoint (not foreseeing just how good she would be at it), they also accepted the first American envoy, a middle-aged political appointee, Townshend Harris. Harris, the Japanese who tried to cope with him, and the little town of Shimoda where he lived all kept day-to-day records and the counterpoint makes delightful reading. Rarely has mutual misunderstanding been so complete. The Japanese were very frustrating to the poor, befuddled man but they were also very polite and, among other amenities, supplied him with a young and beautiful mistress. For her heroic sacrifice in stifling her natural repugnance toward a horrible-looking westerner, all light-colored and hairy, and for performing a great service for her country, Okichi has been much celebrated in Japanese poetry and song.

But I have happy news. The eye of the beholder, everywhere, grows gentler as it grows more sophisticated, as the world, thanks to television and air travel, draws closer together into its global village. Old books and old movies grate on us because of their blatant racism and their rejection of those with physical flaws. We have become more aware of the person and are less preoccupied by the frame. For example, I sometimes don't remember whether a person is black or white, as if this distinction has ceased to make any striking difference. And it's unbelievable to us now that people were once generally ostracized for looking Irish.

These changing attitudes are very clear in rehabilitation of the physically impaired. The old-style cripple usually expected to be, and was, barred from employment, independence, companionship, love, marriage and children. Today's militant young disabled have every intention of being part of the living, learning, working, loving world. And if the world isn't enlightened, they'll set out to enlighten it. Twenty years ago, sex was a dirty word in rehabilitation, but now rehabilitation-style porno movies are shown to demonstrate whatever technical modifications in the joy of sexing may be necessary because of a disability.

As physical flaws become familiar to us as part of a total personality, they often fade into insignificance. Television, by bringing famous people into our living rooms (with 19-inch faces), often forces us to gaze upon the unvarnished truth. We become engrossed in the person. We accept, for example, the sadness of seeing a once breathtakingly handsome actor now old and wrinkled but now also a real person talking of his life, his career, and his adventures, and we accept the flaws of age in exchange for the privilege of deeper acquaintance.

This familiarity has brought changes in our attitudes toward physical appearance so significant that many actors don't bother with camouflage as they would once have done. A very popular young actor, for example, has never bothered to remove a conspicuous mole. Even the commercials are catching up with the rest of us. The women who rave about paper towels and self-cleaning ovens aren't as flawless as they once were.

But having coped with cultures, nationalities, and television trends, we come to the worst hassle of all appearance-wise. Because of some odd bit of childhood conditioning or a stray association tucked away in the murkier depths of the unconscious mind, each of us has our own pet likes and dislikes. You are almost certain to remind a new acquaintance of somebody he's known before (like, God forbid, his first wife). If a hundred people were asked to complete these two sentences: "The physical appearance I dislike most is _____" and "I know it's kind of weird but the physical characteristics that turn me on are _____," heaven knows what replies would result. There's a girl I know who thinks the pimples on the back of her suave, handsome man-of-the-world are kind of cute; there was a man who used to hang around the rehabilitation center trying to pick up girls in wheelchairs; and I know one girl who won't go out with tall men and another one who won't go out with short ones.

So you might as well give up second-guessing and let other people decide whether you strike them as attractive. And, of course, everybody I find attractive has some physical aspect I consider unbeautiful in itself. So I figure nobody has to love my looks. Just let them love me! But if you've absolutely got to be attractive and it's a morning when you hate your bathroom mirror, consider maybe you've just got a phobia against you today, and maybe somebody else will have better taste. And if worst comes to worst, there's always your surgeon. He may appreciate you, for as the great English physiologist J. D. S. Haldane enthused, "The ugliest exterior may contain the most beautiful viscera."

As we have shown, small, funny-looking, stammering, ugly, or crippled people may lead good, full lives despite their physical imperfections. They may do heroic deeds, make pots of money, paint masterpieces, create beautiful music, win great battles, think brilliant thoughts, and marry wonderful mates. They just can't be Don Juans, great lovers. Everybody knows that. Especially Madison Avenue. The men that make the blood zip through a woman's veins are tall and ruggedly handsome. They have all their hair. And their own beautiful white teeth. Their eyes are never crossed. Their ears don't stick out at funny angles. And they never have acne. Of course not.

Scientists have measured the zip through a woman's anatomy at the sight of different kinds of men, with cardiograph, plethysmograph, and sweat meter. The men you see on television mooning over newly Claireled ladies or in *The Fashions of The Times* looking rich and outdoorsy (if terribly narcissistic) are the results of all the charting and analyzing of women's glands. They are all tall, lean, beautifully groomed, and obviously deodorized to a fare-thee-well.

Rasputin, who cut a sexual swath through the Imperial Court of Russia, through an aristocracy of ladies accustomed to beauty, grace, grandeur, and culture in the era of Nijinsky, Pavlova, and Stravinsky, was not quite like that. For starters, he had a stench worse than a goat. He was coarse, drunken, almost illiterate. He had long stringy hair stiff with grease and dirt; a thick black beard encrusted with garbage; unspeakably dirty hands with black fingernails. His filth and smell were indescribable. Stomachs turned as he guzzled his food, dipping his filthy hands in the fish stew in his haste to retrieve the more succulent morsels.

His sales pitch was pure theology. He was a simple, humble peasant, a holy man of God, seeking only the salvation of souls. For salvation one must be redeemed from one's sins; for redemption one must have sins worth being redeemed from. Come, daughter, and I will help you to sin for the sake of heaven.

The line worked phenomenally well, and the ladies rationalized that his coarseness must indeed be a mark of the highest spirituality for, if he weren't holy, would *they* be submitting to him? To a rough peasant? Certainly not. Obviously he was a holy man, and fornicating with him constituted a godly deed.

In his boyhood back in Siberia, his method had been more direct. He grabbed the girls and tore off their clothes. While often mauled in the process, he found the approach on the whole effective. Then he happened upon a most compatible monastery which preached sexual abandonment as the path to God. It met Rasputin's spiritual needs exactly. He soon became a compelling preacher with a growing reputation for miracles.

His reputation as a healer brought him to the attention of royalty. The heir to the throne, the only son of Nicholas and Alexandra, had inherited hemophilia through his great-grandmother, Queen Victoria. When Rasputin was brought to the boy's bedside and relieved the child's torment by his soothing, hypnotic presence, the empress knew that Rasputin was truly a man of God.

From that moment, she was his champion against all enemies, a loyalty that was to kill Rasputin, the csar, Alexandra herself, the child over whom she agonized, and all the other members of the royal family.

So Rasputin was launched into the highest circles of Moscow society, startling and intriguing it with his coarse barnyard language and crude peasant stories, and his mixture of lust and holiness. His sexual conquests began. Noble ladies, actresses, wives of absent officers, and lower-class women found his rough manner wonderfully thrilling. You couldn't call it love-making, for it seemed to be merely an action carried out with a woman's body; it mattered little whose body it happened to be, although he showed a preference for the young and pretty. There is no record of his forming close personal relationships with any of them.

He was a tremendous sexual athlete and lost no time in dalliance. Even so, the offers were more than he could handle. Women swarmed to his apartment, lining the stairway to await their turn. As he sat surrounded, he would talk about souls, perhaps holding a young girl on his lap, or fondling the woman seated next to him. If she were to be chosen, he would rise and lead her into the Holy of Holies (to the undevout, his bedroom). He would, if necessary, lull her qualms by explaining that he was cleansing, not defiling, her. Often such reassurance was not needed.

In 1911, he had set out to seduce a nun. When she proved uncooperative, he attempted to rape her. This deed so outraged the bishop of Hermogen and a fiery monk-priest named Iliodor, who had introduced Rasputin to Moscow, that they made him swear on a holy icon to stay away from women and the Imperial family. For emphasis, Iliodor punched him and crowned him with a large wooden cross. Rasputin swore devoutly, recovered swiftly, and ran to the empress with a much sanctified version. The bishop was punished by banishment to a monastery. Iliodor, who was made of sterner stuff, refused seclusion, attempted a revolution (but was discovered), fled to Finland, wrote a muckraking book about Rasputin, and departed for New York and an American publisher. (And also to employment as a janitor at the Metropolitan Life Insurance Company on Madison Square.)

Meanwhile, between 1914 and 1918, Rasputin was adding great political power to his sexual prowess and religious fervor. The empress had become the power be-

hind the throne and Rasputin had become the voice behind the empress.

A squad of city police was assigned the double task of
spying on and guarding him. They wrote it all down word
for word: "The wife of a Captain of the 145th Hussars
slept at Rasputin's. . . . Rasputin locked a prostitute in
his rooms. The servants let her out." He held drunken
orgies, and started drunken melees even in the most luxu-
rious restaurants. Bruce Lockhart, the British journalist
and consul, happened to be present once when Rasputin
exposed himself and shouted that he often behaved that
way in front of the csar and could do what he liked with
"the Old Girl" (Alexandra).

Yet Rasputin managed to keep his double image to the
end. To the royal family, he was a gentle, saintly, humble
man of God; to the people, a drunken, unclean beast. The
people of Russia knowing nothing of the terrible illness of
her child and Alexandra's agonizing fear that he would die
without Rasputin's intervention, assumed that his hold
over the empress was a debauched one.

Finally, a small group of young nobles deciding, quite
rightly, that Rasputin was destroying the monarchy, determined to murder him, which they proceeded to do
most gruesomely, in what has to be the funniest assassination in history. Although they certainly didn't intend it to
be funny—or gruesome. Quite the contrary. Their design
was most fastidious.

Rasputin was to be lured to a party at the Mocha Palace of young Prince Felix Yousoupov. He would be informed that the princess wished a private audience with
him before the party. As the princess was very beautiful it
was thought that Rasputin would never be able to resist
such an invitation. (Please note that the princess herself

was not on this occasion or on any other involved in any way with Rasputin. The Yousoupovs, later in exile, did rather well from libel suits against movies and books that implied that Rasputin had been killed by the prince to avenge his wife's honor.) The plan called for Rasputin to be led to a room in the cellar to await the assignation, fed poison, and the body disposed of. The room would be well furnished to lull the victim's suspicions. When Russia's richest prince (he was also its handsomest) furnished a cellar, he did it well, with a magnificent Persian rug, inlaid ebony cabinets, ancient embroideries, a sixteenth-century crystal crucifix of the finest Italian workmanship—and, of course, delectable cakes, each with enough poison to kill several men instantly.

The event went off like clockwork, up to a point. The holy man arrived on schedule, the party of four accomplices was sounding much like a party of thirty, aided by the tune of "Yankee Doodle" played loudly on the gramophone to give an air of gaiety and abandon. The host escorted his guest to the cellar and graciously offered refreshments. Rasputin gobbled down two cakes and found them delicious. Not falling dead promptly as planned, he was offered Madeira wine, also spiked with poison. He gulped down two glasses of that and found it very refreshing. Rasputin called for music, insisting that the prince sing and play the guitar for him. After two and a half hours of this impromptu musicale, the prince fell apart (he was, after all, young, and it was his first murder), and rushed upstairs for advice. The upstairs lot proved to be in poor shape too. One conspirator, a physician, had already fainted once. Grand Duke Dmitry suggested, quite sensibly, that they give up and go home.

Yousoupov steeled himself, went back down, and shot

Rasputin in the back. Dr. Lazvert pronounced him dead. At this pronouncement, the corpse arose foaming at the mouth, jumped to its feet, and roaring with fury, chased its murderers up the stairs. Then the quiet little affair got really noisy. The victim broke out of the palace, shouting, "I'll tell everything to the empress. I'll tell everything to the empress." The assassins were so shaken they couldn't have hit a barn door but they kept firing until a bullet, more or less by accident, found its mark. They were by this time terrified, and struck the body again and again hysterically before binding it thoroughly and pushing it into the Neva through a hole in the ice. Rasputin's body was found with arm upraised in his favorite icon pose. After all the poisoning, gunning, and clobbering, he had drowned while attempting to free himself from the rope.

After Rasputin, practically anybody comes as a breath of fresh air, and Byron was not only washed but very, very handsome (short and a little inclined to fat but still breathtaking). His dark, romantic eyes; the perfect, lordly profile (as a matter of fact, he'd been a lord since he was ten); his gracefully curling locks (assisted only a little by sleeping in curl papers), all combined with his virile poetry to drive women mad with desire. But what *really* got to them was that in the midst of all that perfection, he had a grave flaw—a twisted foot—which provided a tragic aura to heat the heart's cockles of any lady addicted to the Gothic novel. (Byron himself fancied his tragic, romantic image and disapproved of his bust done by the Danish sculptor, Thorvaldsen. "It doesn't look at all like me," he said fretfully; "my expression is more unhappy.")

Contessa Guiccioli, Byron's final love, thought other people exaggerated the deformity and said that he had always mounted a horse with remarkable elegance, and played games with dexterity (she hinted at equal dexterity in lovemaking). Since she had bathed his feet on at least one occasion, when he returned overtired from a walk, it seems probable that Byron overreacted to his disability. But with less bitterness would he have been as fascinating?

Because of his flawed body, he could treat women as cruelly as did Heathcliff or be as obnoxious as *Jane Eyre's* Mr. Rochester or *Rebecca's* Maxim de Winter, and the ladies forgave and continued to adore.

Since they had never met his atrocious mother, or heard of his father, "Mad Jack," or his great-uncle, "Wicked Lord Byron," they ascribed everything to his crippled foot and excused everything because of it. And there was a good deal to excuse. Although he *was* kind to animals.

His huge, ferocious-looking bulldog, Smut, accompanied him to the university. When the rules expelled the dog, Byron consoled himself by installing a large, good-natured bear, to stroll with him through the streets of Cambridge. (The university had not thought to rule out bears.)

At both Harrow and Cambridge, young Byron lived up to the profligacy of his male ancestors very well. Despite his many refreshing trips to London's social whirl, university life palled. He left Cambridge for the City.

From London he soon wrote happily, and probably quite accurately, to a friend still moldering at college: "I am buried in an abyss of sensuality."

He next set out to tour the Continent. When traveling, he habitually assaulted chambermaids. At Malta, he had an agreeable affair with a married English lady. In Athens, he took a twelve-year-old, whose mother first tried for marriage but settled finally for renting the girl. Byron grew very fond of this Teresa and would have taken her away with him except her grasping parent wanted 30,000 piastres, so Byron contended himself with writing a poem:

> Maid of Athens, ere we part,
> Give, oh give me back my heart!
> Or since that has left my breast,
> Keep it now, and take the rest!
> Hear my vow before I go,
> Ζωή μου, σᾶς α γᾶπ ῶ.

(Don't worry about translating the Greek. Whatever he vowed, he never kept it.) He arrived back in England with four thousand more lines of poetry. *Childe Harold*'s fiery, red-blooded poetry and its stormy, romantic author burst like a rocket on the bored, ultra-sophisticated, utterly immoral London society. As the Duchess of Devonshire put it: "*Childe Harold* is on every table, and himself courted, visited, flattered, and praised whenever he appears . . . in short, he is really the only topic of conversation—the men jealous of him, the women of each other."

While the ladies didn't line up on his staircase as they had on Rasputin's, their carriages carrying invitations clogged the street on which he lived. He was a transient in the bed of so many highly born and gratifyingly low-moraled ladies that there's no more keeping track of them than of his progress of chambermaids on his travels. But two or three were more than transient, and one exiled him from England forever.

When Lady Caroline Lamb first set eyes on him, she wrote in her diary: "Mad—bad—dangerous to know" (a description almost equally applicable to Caroline herself), but prophesied, "that pale face is my fate." And so it was, for a while. They embarked on a furious, outrageously public affair, while her husband merely seemed entertained by the spectacle. But Lady Caroline set a pace that even Byron could not hold. She also proved very sticky to ditch. But after a scene in which Caroline tried to stab herself, Byron cooled off in a quiet affair with the Countess of Oxford, whose husband was even more understanding than Caroline's, having had even more experience. The lady's children were known to London society as the "Miscellany" because of their assorted fathers. (She seems not to have added a little Byron to the collection.)

Then his half-sister, Augusta, arrived in town, handsome, sexually exciting, and fun—and without her husband. Byron, who had never let a scruple interfere with an amorous impulse in his life, was infatuated. But this affair gave him enough pause to disturb his sleep.

He settled the problem, or thought he had, by marrying high-minded and prudish, but wealthy Annabella Milbanke. This immediately drove him to drink, and he finally turned back to sister Augusta, who was a great deal more fun. Annabella ultimately decided Byron was insane, did not care at all for the idea of incest, picked up their infant daughter, and left; Byron never saw either of them again.

But the moment Annabella had departed, Byron wanted her back. He wrote fervent love letters. Annabella merely consulted her lawyer. Byron wrote a reproachful, wronged-husband poem. He drank a lot and returned to other women.

Finally, he took his half-sister, Augusta, to a very fashionable ball in a highly interesting and very visible condition. The ladies present, presuming him to be responsible for Augusta's state, turned and swept out of the ballroom one by one. It seemed one sin was too dark even for this profligate society.

Byron was so enraged by the insult that he fled England to spend the rest of his life in Italy. But first he stopped off in Switzerland long enough to get Shelley's sister-in-law pregnant, be present at the conception of Mary Shelley's *Frankenstein* (which has probably made more money than all the poets since time began), and to talk about poetry. The two poets, the great Byron and the fledgling Shelley, enormously enjoyed talking shop. They had a high regard for one another's work, very different from Byron's opinion of some other poets. He considered Wordsworth, for example, one of those sickly sentimental lyrical poets, and as for Johnny Keats and his "piss a bed" poetry: "John Keats or Ketch, or whatever his names are: why, his is the Onanism of poetry. . . . I don't mean he is *indecent*, but viciously soliciting his own ideas into a state which is neither poetry nor any thing else but a bedlam vision produced by raw pork and opium." (Apparently, around poets, it is even more hazardous to be a fellow poet than to be an ex-lover.)

After the Shelley ménage had departed, Byron continued on his way to Venice and the twenty-two-year-old wife of his landlord. "I have fallen in love," he wrote, "which, next to falling into the canal . . . is the best or the worst thing, I could do. . . ." Of course he didn't limit himself to Marianna. How could one in Venice? At Carnival time? He received a letter informing him that he and Claire Claremont had a daughter. He instructed that the child was to be called Allegra and proceeded with some serious reveling. In fact, he reveled so thoroughly that he came down with a fever which apparently made him feel every one of his twenty-eight years, for he wrote that geriatric poem

> So we'll go no more a-roving
> So late into the night
> Though the heart be still as loving
> And the moon be still as bright.

His roving abilities soon returned. Quite spectacularly. But first he replaced Marianna with the wife of a baker. She was, wrote Byron, "fit to breed gladiators from." Soon she had the household well in hand. Thieving tradesmen had been screamed into scrupulosity and lazy servants had been suitably beaten. Even Byron was put in some awe. She was the only woman he ever met who could match him for temper. Their quarrels were magnificent. Yet, while she might scream at him, she also pampered and mothered him (probably the best mother Byron ever had).

And she saw no cause to fuss over his sexual escapades. She knew he would always come back to her. And that year at Carnival he really let loose, more flamboyantly licentious than any Venetian. His reputation had spread. Women were eager to see if the tales of his lovemaking were really true. The parade was endless and totally indiscriminate: great ladies and harlots, wives and virgins. He delighted in intriguing behind husbands' backs (once he clung to a palazzo window for nearly an hour) and seducing daughters under the noses of stern fathers. Once on his way to an assignation, he fell into the canal but went anyway, dripping wet. He liked to swim home occasionally along the canal, pushing a lantern on a board to light his path. He became a tourist attraction, his notoriety even reaching to England. One day in Rome Lady

Liddell saw him and wrote of the experience: "And what came over me I cannot describe, but I felt ready to sink, and stood as if my feet were rooted to the ground, looking at him . . . as if I were horror struck." But not too immobilized to rescue her daughter, Maria, telling her to keep her eyes down. "Don't look at him, he is dangerous to look at." (One hopes Maria got one little glimpse and did not have to spend the rest of her life wondering what it would have done to her if she had looked.)

Visitors to Venice paid their gondoliers to take them past the Palazzo Mocenigo that they might gaze at the scene of the wild Lord Byron's orgies, for ordinary lecheries had begun to pall. He began to pay gondoliers to bring new and more exotic companions to the Grand Bedroom (including perhaps themselves?).

The baker's wife did last a long time. Byron hated to tell her to go finally, but she had become impossibly domineering. He was gentle and firm (very different from the way he behaved with silly infatuated girls or troublesome wives). La Fornarina couldn't take him seriously until he became stern and ordered her to leave. Then she went quietly. Far too quietly.

She returned like a tornado. When a servant tried to shut the door, she smashed it open. Byron was carving a roast when she sprang into the dining room and seized the carving knife. Byron managed to subdue her, although he got cut in the process. Her defiance broke and she left. Next her body was pulled from the canal and she was deposited, dripping, at his feet. She was put to bed, and when she recovered, once more Byron explained patiently and gently. This time she understood and went away for good.

His next favorite was a young-in-spirit countess of

sixty. The Countess Benzoni had a voice like a foghorn and gave off a nourishing aroma of garlic from the hot rolls she sometimes secreted in her bosom as she gondola-ed from ball to ball. But her place in Byron's story is because of an introduction. He was very, very tired of women and wanted to avoid them, "If they are ugly, because they are ugly. If they are pretty, because they are pretty." Then the Countess presented him to Teresa Guiccioli, nineteen-year-old wife of a fifty-eight-year-old husband. She was to be his woman for the rest of his short life. If she had been free, they probably would have married, and when he lost interest it was not because of another woman but for Greece's struggle for liberation.

This was a basically stable, domestic relationship, but a stable relationship à la Byron is not quite like a stable relationship chez you or me.

The first act contained a Shakespearean cast of characters including, among numerous others, the young contessa's father, a spy on behalf of her husband, the Pope, the Italian Liberation Army, Byron's illegitimate little daughter Aurora, and a large menagerie that had to be relocated along with nursemaids, other servants, and furniture at various stages in the plot. The animals consisted, according to a list provided by Shelley, of "ten horses, eight enormous dogs, three monkeys, five cats, an eagle, a crow, and a falcon; and all these, except the horses, walk about the house, which every now and then resounds with their unarbitrated quarrels, as if they were masters of it." Then he added, "I find that my enumeration of the animals . . . was defective. . . . I have just met on the grand staircase, five peacocks, two guinea hens and an Egyptian crane." In addition to Shelley's roster, four ducks bought by Byron for a St. Michaelmas dinner so endeared themselves that they could not be consumed, and joined the caravan, fitting neatly, if not quietly, under the driver's seat.

As for the ensuing acts, suffice it to say that this already stable relationship eventually simmered down to a life within normal limits for any rich, exotic English lord contending with a noble, Italian mistress; a wronged husband who wanted to be compensated for his loss; the even more wronged mother of his child; a large menagerie; a revolution, Italian-style; a very good friend named Shelley with a passion for boats equaled only by his indiscretions in seamanship, and, as a consequence, a funeral pyre on the beach which one is required to attend; and, finally, a fatal urge to rush off and liberate Greece from the Turks.

But before Byron could engage the enemy, he fell ill. As long as he was conscious he fought the doctors off from killing him with their bloodletting, saying, "The lancet has killed more people than the lance." He didn't really care much. He had lived so greedily, his life was all used up. He said, "Few men can live faster than I did. I am, literally speaking, a young old man." He was thirty-six.

His body was returned to England, the coffin submerged in a cask of alcohol. The bells of Westminster tolled for his funeral, the cortege was led by the riderless State Horse, followed by the carriages of England's nobility. But the profligate society of London had not even now forgiven his scandal. Their carriages were empty except for the pages. Only the people of London lined the route and choked the narrow streets.

The Don Juan of the seventeenth century had been Antoine Nompar de Caumont, who from his adventures and intrigues also emerged as the Marquis de Penguilon and, finally, as the Duc de Lanzin. He was "one of the smallest men God ever made," and his hair was greasy and never combed. But he had *"la belle jambe."* And in a period of tight breeches, a good leg was not an asset to be taken lightly.

His character, like his appearance, was a very mixed bag. He was eccentric, avaricious, witty, jealous, and vicious, an ambitious malcontent always knee-deep in intrigue, but capable of faithful friendship, wild generosity, and extreme bravery. When this wild mixture of good and evil came up to Paris from the provinces with no money but phenomenal self-confidence, it almost immediately wrought havoc among the ladies of the French court, including the much older cousin of the king, that formidable institution, La Grande Mademoiselle. Soon everybody at the court, including King Louis XIV himself, was a little afraid of de Caumont.

When one of his mistresses, the Princess de Monaco, was unfaithful to him, he "accidentally" stomped on her hand with his high heel. Once when feuding with that most hateful of Louis' mistresses, Madame de Montespan, he hid under the royal bed and listened while she and the king talked about his intrigues. As with many other eavesdroppers, what he heard made him furious. In fact, the bugging threw him into such a rage that he confronted the pair, for which he was first thrown into the Bastille, then exiled with an out-of-Paris appointment.

He responded by engaging himself to La Grande Mademoiselle (she probably has a name but nobody ever mentions it). This annoyed Louis even more and he threw the miscreant back into the Bastille—this time for ten years. He is believed to have married the aging lady anyway (but very discreetly). When she died, he prudently transferred to the English court and carried on his amatory, political, and military ventures with continuing gusto, but apparently more caution, since he did not end up in the Tower of London.

But the hot-shot among the great lovers is, of course, Giovanni Jacopo Casanova de Seingalt, a real Casanova with the ladies, at least four hundred of them he calculated by the time he wrote his memoirs. But then he had an advantage. He had grown up in the Venice of the early eighteenth century, the ideal time and place for all four of his careers—writer, scholar, scoundrel, lover.

To Venetians—patricians, workmen, scholars, bishops, monks and nuns—the senses were a gift of God and He expected that people would gratify them.

But while Casanova's city was exactly right for a budding Great Lover, his appearance decidedly was not. He had been, somebody found it noteworthy enough to record, "the ugliest baby that ever lived." While he outgrew the worst and became a tall, well-built man with a swagger, the nose remained far too much nose to combine gracefully with a receding chin and a receding forehead. The best the Prince de Ligne could find to say was, "He would be a handsome man were he not ugly."

Casanova became one of the most cosmopolitan men in history—a doctor of law and theology, with wider medical knowledge than the average physician (he sometimes regretted he had never become one), and an insatiable thirst for learning which never left him.

But above all else he grew up licentious. Rasputin was driven by lust and madness, Byron by cynicism, and the legendary Don Juan by hatred of women—conquering only to triumph and degrade; but Casanova enjoyed women immensely. And his hundreds of women remembered him with pleasure and affection. When in his wandering he met them again, the reunions were warm and festive.

In the eighteenth century love was a sport, and Casanova played the game magnificently. He was very virile and never lost his excitement at the prospect of a liaison, any more, he explained, than one tires of the infinite variety of books. And he sampled all kinds from titled ladies to scullery maids—of any age, so long as they had charm. He was not at all demanding that she be beautiful. "A book may," he noted, from wide experience of both women and books, "be better than its title page suggests."

Casanova enjoyed giving pleasure, being attentive, anticipating a women's desires, spending money lavishly to entertain her, and, if need be, to clothe her beautifully. But perhaps most of all, he valued the spiritual side of a relationship. Women interested him as people. He loved to talk with his paramours (for which, no doubt, women then, as now, were truly grateful).

He once declined one of England's top courtesans because he didn't speak the language, and "without speech the pleasure is diminished two thirds." He was amoral but not insensitive. He would not, for example, take a woman unless the passion were mutual.

He took care of his loves and was concerned for their welfare and their futures, often marrying them off to their advantage. He befriended women "in trouble," one of them a nun, and one of them Justine Wynne, a writer of repute and daughter of an English baronet.

In the course of several hundred amatory encounters, some the pleasure of a single hour, some prolonged love affairs (he came close to marriage on two or three occasions), he built up a formidable expertise, an expertise perhaps not completely useful again to aspiring Don Juans until our own bawdy era.

Sex was a need of life, like food and drink, and taken with little more soul-searching or scruple. Beds à trois were not unusual. You'd never have thought them wicked enough to be called orgies, just jolly little get-togethers, judging by the one Casanova shared with a Neapolitan's wife and her sister.

In fact, in his *Memoirs*, which give many timely hints to seducers, Casanova explained that it's easier to succeed with hesitant girls if you approach them two at a time. They are, he found, less timid, each made more daring by the daring of the other. As he put it: "In my long and profligate career, I have become familiar with all the methods of seduction; but my guiding principle never has been to direct any attack against those whose prejudices were likely to prove an obstacle, except in the presence of another woman." And his methods worked in all the countries of Europe but one—England.

That wretched country was his downfall, its women beyond his comprehension. A London woman of high social position offered Casanova a place in her carriage. Naturally they broke the monotony of their journey by love-making, but later at a ball she pretended not to know him. "Folly," she said, looking down her nose at the much annoyed Casanova, "does not carry with it a claim to acquaintance."

A leading courtesan, La Charpillon, took malacious pleasure in defeating a gallant so renowned for his amours. She literally drove him crazy, to the verge of suicide.

His misfortunes deepened. Her costly wooing had required much replenishing of capital. Casanova had always made most of his money by gambling but this time he gambled with an opponent who gave him a bad check and skipped town. When Casanova attempted to cash it, he had to flee the country to escape hanging—the penalty for this offense.

But, as Casanova complained, the English are a people much too serious. True, other countries had jailed him from time to time and given him the trouble of breaking out. But hanging! The whole deplorable experience told on the middle-aged Casanova and he retreated from the arena of love to devote the rest of his life to his *Memoirs*, the finest social history we have of the times in which he lived. He had lived decently, according to his standards. (When he was having much success with the ladies, he took it as a sign that God was helping him.) He had been careful not to be a sexual exploiter, nor a downright thief. A little bit of a crook, maybe, but dishonest, no. "Cheating is wrong but honest deceit is nothing but prudence. It is a virtue . . . who does not practice it is a fool."

And he, who had begun as a priest (and an eloquent preacher except for that once at the age of sixteen when he showed up in the pulpit very intoxicated), summed himself up: "I have lived a philosopher. . . . I die a Christian."

Legend insists that even death did not completely subdue Casanova. The metal cross on his grave caught and entangled the skirts of women as they passed on their way to church.

And where Casanova failed with the heartless La Charpillon, John Wilkes succeeded particularly well. But this was nothing unusual for Wilkes. He was one of the most profligate men of the era and probably one of the ugliest, with a terrible cross-eyed squint and a face horribly scarred by smallpox. When the staid *Encyclopaedia Britan-*

nica says somebody is ugly, you'd better believe it, and John Wilkes was remarkably ugly—and remarkably fascinating. An interesting man on all counts, without the slightest hesitation in tackling City Hall, Wilkes fought for parliamentary reform and the grievances of the American colonies as well as those of the lower classes of England. He attacked George III with such effect that even the seven-year-old Prince of Wales was inspired to write a seditious slogan on his father's bedroom door, thereby becoming one of the earliest of the king's rebellious subjects. Wilkes was thrown out of Parliament, imprisoned, and then marooned in France for years, not daring to return to London for fear of further imprisonment. While he always had found time for sexual encounters (he even belonged to a secret society dedicated to obscenity), the exile in France allowed him to devote himself fully to amours. (So admired was he by the American colonists that an actor by the name of Junius Booth named a younger son in his honor, a son destined to attack a ruler with bullets as well as words.)

But Casanova and John Wilkes lived before the days of the Hollywood image. They'd probably never have made it in an era when women were swooning over the classic profiles of John Gilbert and John Barrymore; dying of grief over Rudolph Valentino; and longing to share a tumbrel to the guillotine with the wonderful dark eyes and thrilling voice of Ronald Colman.

Then imagine a short guy with a face not likely to appeal to a mother, rabbity teeth, grating voice, fuzzy lisp, altogether the kind that women raised on movie stars never bother with. I don't think the studios ever figured out what happened to women when they met Humphrey Bogart on the screen (or, apparently, off it), but the film makers loved what he did to female desires as reflected at the box office. And young men to this day watch reruns of Bogart's old movies in hopes of absorbing his raspy voice and tough manner by way of upgrading their sex appeal, while John Gilbert seems about as stimulating as a department store dummy.

So Madison Avenue, what do you make of women now with their conglomeration of lovers? Where are your handsome faces, with the deep, resonant male voices? Too busy selling shaving cream to have time for women?

And what advice can we give an ordinary sixteen-year-old driven to heights of amorous ambition by *Playboy* and his latest purchase of pornography? Can we offer him hope even if he isn't ugly, his teeth and eyes don't cross, he isn't maniacally religious, and he isn't undersized? He can't even go around encrusted with filth because his mother keeps washing his clothes. What's to do? Let him not despair. You never can tell what women will go ape over. There may be simply hordes waiting eagerly for even a well-favored youth without physical imperfections.

The Moral
of It All

W'E'VE TALKED ABOUT many physical imperfections. But which of these imperfections were truly flaws?

When, in 1936, a certain country gentleman was informed that he had fallen heir to the greatest empire the world had ever seen, his first royal act was to burst into tears. Considering that his ancestors had fought, pillaged, and committed most of the more gruesome crimes (including infanticide) to seize this bloody crown, the reaction of King George VI seems rather odd. But not to him. Not only had he not, in the best old English tradition, plotted to murder his brother, the king, but he begged Edward VIII, for God's sake, to keep the wretched headgear. He, himself, wanted to go on being as obscure a country squire as a royal son can be. He had not the slightest wish to make his amiable wife queen or to secure the succession for his children, adored and adorable as they might be.

(His ancestor, Henry VIII, had toppled the Roman Catholic Church in Britain and murdered well and often to secure the same throne for his son.) But in no way did George VI want to be king. For how can a man be a king if every time he opens his mouth he sounds like a bumbling idiot? A modern king of England who stutters! And who has to follow a charming, very verbal brother. Every time George, or rather Bertie (he even had to have a new, kingly name for his new role), was forced to say a few words at a regimental display or the opening of a charity bazaar, he was in an agony of embarrassment. The newsreels showed him clearly why there were rumors he was not too bright. As king he would have to make many speeches—to the whole world. He would even have to stumble through a coronation broadcast. He could not do it. But, of course, he did. One does what one must.

Now history, including your personal history and mine, is a very unpredictable matter. We often do not know which events in our lives are good or bad until a long time afterward. There are even those who believe that *all* things work together for good if accepted as some great pattern of life, and we must concede that some of the best things in our lives happened as a direct consequence of some of the worst things in our lives. A lost job or a lost love is often a prelude to a better career or a better love.

And so it was with George VI and his stammer. His biographers would rank that impediment as one of his finest assets for the job that lay ahead. And vice versa. The job almost cured the stuttering. This is how it all worked out. The Empire was aware of the new king's affliction, and the first radio encounter between king and commoner was a very queasy affair. Like worried parents at their offspring's first music recital, his subjects anx-

iously negotiated every treacherous polysyllable with him
(like millions of stage prompters), and held their breath
with every hesitation.

And so began the warm bond between his people and
their king-by-default. In fact, George VI was thought to
be an integral part of the remarkable solidarity of the British Empire during World War II. Of all the nations, only
his colonies never cooperated with or betrayed to the
enemy, no matter how they might fight for independence
in times of peace. At home, his quiet, courageous presence
comforted the people as he visited them among their
bombed-out houses. (His own was an especially desirable
target to the Germans, who hit Buckingham Palace many
times.) And in the years that Britain and her Com-
monwealth stood alone against the might of Hitler, his
radio greetings could not have sounded more comforting
had he the smooth delivery of the greatest Shakespearean
actor. And when he died in 1952, George VI took his
place as one of the most worthwhile of British sovereigns
and one of its best-loved.

And the combination of dogged practice and the affection of his people finally gave George VI the security a
stammerer needs to speak freely. There even came a time
when his speeches were admired (only a stutterer can appreciate his pleasure in this) for their oratory.

So the first question to be asked about your flaws is:
Are you sure? How do you know they're really flaws?
How much better would your life be without them? Your
fears may be miles away from the truth. Take the Sad
Case of New York City and the Perfect Mayor. It's a
truism in politics that a candidate should be very tall,
charming, and, if possible, handsome. John Lindsay was
all that and then some. On the day he decided to run for

mayor of New York, he was quite the handsomest thing in American, or perhaps any other, politics. And that was only the beginning. He was also intelligent, courageous, compassionate, imaginative, and determined to make New York City work. He promised to turn New York into a paradise of peace, tranquility, and progress as every other candidate, to the instant disbelief of New Yorkers, had been promising since the first mayoralty race in 1534. But when John Lindsay offered to slay dragons for them, him they believed—because he looked so good. And by the end of his tenure they hated him as they had never bothered to hate the assortment of crooks and incompetents who, from time to time, had graced the office of mayor.

The funny thing was, he probably wasn't half bad, just ruined by his looks. Being tall, blond, and beautiful, he stood out in every crowd. When, as always happens in New York, a surprise snowstorm found a third of the snow plows in shop for repairs and the sanitation workers God knows where, the house owners of Queens screamed for blood, specifically Lindsay's. Taxi drivers risked collisions and apoplexy at the mention of his name.

So New York turned John Lindsay in on a very small, physically unnoteworthy senior citizen from whom nobody, except a few other senior citizens, expected any miracles at all. And now when there's a blizzard and it turns out one third of the snow plows are broken and half the sanitation workers are on holiday for the day, nobody at all blames the mayor. We just say to one another, "Nuttin' ever works in this lousy city." In any case, he doesn't stand out in a crowd, and you aren't reminded that he's around and maybe responsible for your particular disaster of the moment. Even when the cameramen find him, they can't get any clear picture because he's difficult to see, and even if they happen to get him in focus, you have to figure out which unnewsworthy mug is his. There are probably television viewers who think the city is being run by a newsman from CBS, not being able to tell the difference.

So if you're hankering to be mayor of New York City and are young, tall, handsome, and aristocratic, forget it. Try Boston or Philadelphia. If you look like St. George, people are going to expect defunct dragons, whereas, if you look like any ordinary slob of a knight, they'll be delighted if you deliver one telling blow, or back the beast off, or, better yet, coax it to move to New Jersey. And if you're shorter than the news reporters and totally indistinguishable, you can probably occupy city hall till the Grim Reaper casts his ballot against you. Remember, New York's patron saint is a man by the name of Fiorello La Guardia, who certainly didn't look like much but was one hell of a good mayor.

All through history, you can find physical disabilities that didn't interfere where you'd expect them to and perfection that did. And I know all kinds of real-life stories. I'm forced to suppose novelists and playwrights don't get around much, psychologically speaking. They seem to think they know what the life consequences of a physical defect will be. I surely don't. For example, I assumed there would be suicidal patients in a rehabilitation center (there were very few). What I didn't expect was the lover who killed himself because his crippled girl friend was going to leave him for another man. You expect newly disabled people will sometimes get Dear John letters and occasionally they do. You don't foresee you have to cope with husbands frantic because while they'd been home working themselves to death to raise the money, and coping valiantly with diaper rash and mothers-in-law, their wives are living it up at the rehabilitation center, falling madly in love with fellow patients, and demanding divorces.

Or the vocational counseling that proved totally unnecessary because the patient, who was paraplegic, promptly got a husband to support her, and when bored with him moved on to a Latin lover and let him take over her support. (And what *able-bodied* woman, in this day and age, manages to get supported by a Latin or any other lover?) You're not surprised when a disabled woman complains bitterly that her men friends find her fascinating, they even love her; they just never desire her. But the next one complains that men are interested only in her body and she gets sick of having to fend off passes.

So if you think you know the consequences of your flaws, don't be surprised if life surprises you. (Unless, of course, you've hopelessly stacked the cards by your attitudes.)

I know a woman who was born with large facial growths which when removed left her badly scarred for life. When she was two years old, she had polio which paralyzed both legs. She still walks with crutches. Now, I'm sure she once despaired over her disabilities and disfigurement, thinking they would spoil her life. I'm sure they sometimes made life very difficult for her. I'm sure they cause her daily aggravation now. But spoil her life? Well, not quite! I know very few people who live as well. She is highly valued in her profession; socially, the most welcome of guests. When challenged as to whether I know of any really good marriages, I immediately think of hers. Good lovers, good companions, and good friends, she and her husband have one of the pleasantest homes I know. They even agree on such divisive issues as house buying and adventurous travel. (She does complain about crutches in Venice. The sidewalks are terrible.)

There's a big difference between a flawed body and a flawed life. So if you've got some conspicuous or troublesome defect, let's be hardboiled about it. How much *need* it hamper you from attaining your goals in life? How much may it interfere? Need it be a serious flaw at all? Probably not—if you're smart. Consider a good actor. No matter what he looks like, he can be convincing in almost any role because he looks at himself realistically, even ruthlessly, and adapts the role to himself. Let's take Lord Laurence Olivier, Charles Laughton, Paul Newman, Peter Ustinov, Rex Harrison, Orson Welles, George C. Scott and Marlon Brando. All kinds of bodies in all degrees of perfection and imperfection. Yet each could play the role of romantic lover and make it completely believable with a style and an approach that fitted his face, his voice, his body. (History's great lovers were an even more motley crew.) Charles Boyer and Humphrey Bogart just played their Casbah scenes very differently. Some lucky people in ordinary life understand this very well, look their defects squarely in the eye, and find ways of fitting them gracefully into almost any lifestyle they wish to build, although I really don't recommend dueling if you have to use crutches. However, Benjamin Coustau, an eighteenth-century writer and politician, fought a duel sitting down—and won. It might be irrational to plan to be a dancing master if you have two artificial legs. Yet a man by the name of Spinola in the sixteenth century was a very successful one.

So if you're smart you'll look at your flaws, regret them if you must, then see how much living you can do with the rest. The best-dressed women are likely to be the

ones who have ruthlessly come to terms with every limita-
tion of face and form. If you look at people on a crowded
street, you can see how few have done this. Many are
dressed for a figure they don't have, for an age they're not,
and sometimes even for a sex they've never been. They're
like George Eliot, that brilliant, adored, but hopelessly
frumpy lady who topped off her big, sad, homely face
with the frivolous bonnets that rightfully belonged to a
Dolley Madison.

Not that it's easy to look at the clothes with the beautiful lines you'd love to have for the figure you'd also love to
have, and then go off to dress, cheerfully and affec-
tionately, the body you do have. People who are fat have a
particularly hard time with this. If you're short this
month, you know you'll be short next month. But if
you're overweight, maybe you'll stick to your diet and be
thinner within a few weeks and maybe buying something
a size too small will be an inspiration. Besides, isn't it immoral or something to love your fat body and dress it
handsomely? It's a *bad* body. It doesn't deserve to look
good.

So it's almost startling to see a fat person who looks exactly right. I remember a complete stranger who was both
fat and fascinating. No dark, unobtrusive suit tapering
from large abdomen to narrow pant legs to make him look
like a big vase about to topple on a tiny base. This man
evidently had selected his clothes on the premise that if he
were going to be conspicuous, he should be conspicuous
with a flair. First, good, substantial but fashionable shoes
and light-colored slacks in an interesting texture and
weave, and wide at the cuffs. With these, the large struc-
ture had been given a visually solid foundation. It was
topped with a dark brown jacket and eye-catching neck-

wear. The whole effect, in addition to being attractive to the eye, proclaimed a man of substance who thought well of his size and person. An interesting man to know, perhaps.

But few people carry their physical imperfections so cheerfully. In fact, as any psychotherapist can tell you, a great many people with minor imperfections (including psychotherapists!) can be absolutely idiotic about them, and by their idiocy drive themselves and other people to distraction—or to rejection. Then the dumdums sit and complain about what *Fate* has done to them.

I've spared you most of the bitter stories of famous people who, given one handicap by nature or accident, anted it up to a lifetime of misery. But in case you should wish to follow their example, here's the formula (according to a well-known psychologist). First, you have a physical imperfection or an inadequacy of some kind. You then reject yourself because of it. This will make it easy for you to assume that other people are going to reject you too. You picture them rejecting you. This makes you very hostile or afraid of them, so you become very guarded, or self-conscious or disagreeable to somebody who has in reality never done a thing to you and hasn't a glimmer why you're acting the way you are. The encounter then fails because of your orneriness. You, not knowing this, go home more bitter than ever over the world's rejection of you because of your imperfection or inadequacy. This is a time-honored method of getting turned down on job interviews, ignored by the opposite sex, and leading a deliciously self-pitying life. Of course, there's no guarantee you wouldn't have been spurned anyway. But fair's fair. Other people ought to be allowed to write their half of the script; after all, half of the encounter belongs to them.

And if it comes to that, I don't see why they don't have as
much right to reject you as you do.

And in case you think this is a very silly gambit, which
it is, I'll almost guarantee that we'll all use it in some form
or other before the week is out—feeling annoyed with
somebody whom we picture disliking something we cook,
or wear, or say, or do.

So don't assume that every crummy thing that happens
to you is because of your handicap or flaw. The high
school girl with braces on her teeth may figure that's why
she doesn't get dates, and I suppose it's possible—but not
probable.

So ask whether the flaw did it to you or was it merely
bad luck or was it flaw plus your attitude. One way to tell
is to look around and see how other people with the same
flaw are doing. If anybody is making it, then try to figure
out how they do it. And you have to be on the alert for
scapegoating. Like Brutus, we'd rather blame our misfortunes on our flaws, our stars, or anything that proves we
didn't do it ourselves. We hate to take the natural consequences of our behavior. We'll blame anything so long as
it proves we're innocent. It was our looks, our ethnic
group, the awfulness of other people, and, right now, the
stars are taking the rap again. Can we help it if we're a
Gemini, or a Scorpio? While this makes one very innocent
it also makes one very helpless. Sometimes I say briskly to
a complaining husband or wife that I certainly hope the
fault is all their own because then the remedy is within
their own hands. It'll be a lot tougher to correct if the guilt
is all on the other side. But mostly, they don't like this
viewpoint. Better a clear conscience than a resolved marital problem. So if you've got physical defects, and people
are treating you badly, you can, like President John

Adams, decide it's because you're shorter than other people and not because you're a pain in the neck.

The exact truth is that a lot of people who think they
have social or vocational troubles because of their flaws
would have them anyway. And nobody knows better than
a therapist that the physically perfect can louse up their
lives with the worst of us. That is, in fact, very encouraging. The advantaged often live their lives so ineptly that
it's no sweat to keep up to them. But many people with
imperfections refuse to notice or believe this obvious fact.
They really think life would run along like a song if they
lost the weight or the acne. Possibly, yes. Probably, no.

By the way, have you never had the subversive
thought that the plump Before Lady in the reducing ads
looks happier and more likeable than the trim After edi-
tion? Or that the homely woman in the *Ladies' Home Journal*
articles on make-up looks like a totally uninteresting specimen of humanity—a human cliché—when they've finished
prettying her up? I always have a feeling her husband's
probably going to leave the new her. There's a game I
play to find out how I really feel about people's looks. (It's
most enlightening when played by two.) When you see
two people walking together on the street, decide which
one is better-looking. Then decide which of the two you
would prefer for a friend or a lover. I find there is a correlation between what I find attractive and what I think is
beautiful, but much less than I would have guessed. Of
course, you may be more choosey—or less. You may, in
fact, be very hung-up on physical perfection, which is
likely to make you believe everybody is, and that is going
to hurt a lot unless you, yourself, are flawless.

I think of two men that I know. Both care very much
about beauty but one, like many artists, finds it where

others are blind. Much as he may respect and enjoy classical standards, his likes and his loves are chosen for their attractiveness to him. His attitude toward his own physical shortcomings is equally flexible. He may regret them, in passing, but basically he accepts them as part of himself and, therefore, okay. If anybody rejected him because of them (I doubt if anybody has; his self-acceptance makes it improbable), he'd probably shrug and think, "*C'est la vie.*"

To the other, attractive means perfect. You can't imagine him loving a woman who is not beautiful, and he rarely fails to notice other people's imperfections. His demanding standards have made him the bitter enemy of his own body. As he is, in appearance, a very average guy, he has suffered every inch of the way from boyhood acne to middle-aged hairline. If a woman found him devastatingly attractive (as without his nonsense, he might be to a good many, and even is to some in spite of it), he'd either disbelieve it—or reject them for having poor taste!

The number of hours I've spent pounding a few basic truths into assorted numbskulls including my own A typical story goes something like this. Some girl (not that boys have any more sense) gets it into her fool head that she's never going to get a man because she's too fat or her teeth are crooked or her skin breaks out. (Remind me to prescribe an afternoon at the marriage license bureau observing the physiques that achieve her desired goal.) If she were rational on the subject, she would have noticed even within her own circle of acquaintances many exceptions to her gloomy forebodings. To tell the truth, she couldn't tell you, in detail, the physical faults of even her closest friends. My patients, and my friends, carry on about imperfections that are invisible to me until they open my eyes. Then, sure enough, they're a little too plump here, or a little too spotted there, or the hair isn't where it used to be. But it's terribly conceited of them to think I'm going to look them over so carefully. After all, I'm busy with my own nonsense, and, you know, my friends are so blind they can know me for years and not notice certain glaring flaws. Of course, there are some people who get fun out of criticizing other people's defects, but I figure you owe them a flaw or two just to keep them happy. As for worrying about their rejection, it's either a simple aversion to strangers and will wear off, or they're not your type anyway.

You see, we all have a double standard about flaws. We talk one game and play another. We write off people we don't know or don't like by means of careless, even cruel, stereotypes. No prudent crystal ball is going to confront a woman with the image of a short, fat, bald man in her future, even though the same girl one day may ride off happily into the sunset with her very own s, f, b man. If people with flaws understand this double standard and stay in the game, the flaws usually vanish or even, as if by magic, turn into advantages.

As a matter of fact, if your appearance fits any stereotype, you may have to make an extra effort, even if the stereotype is a very positive one. Physically perfect, beautiful people can have bad trouble too if, for any reason, the inside and the outside don't match. Then the inner person risks being neglected and lonely. A woman writer with a deformity wrote that it was like being forced to wear a disguise; that people who would have enjoyed her had no idea she was there. In her case the surprises of closer acquaintance were happy ones, but suppose the reverse is true: the exterior is inviting and the interior is dull or unattractive. Marilyn Monroe suffered acutely from this kind of discrepancy; perhaps, in the long run, it killed her. If the outside woman had matched the frightened, bereft child that Marilyn Monroe felt like, there would have been no gorgeous sex symbol, but perhaps a fine actress playing tragic, problem roles. Then the people drawn to her would have been those who belonged and not people who felt defrauded when they came to know her well. Or more probably, if she had not locked herself into the beautiful disguise, she might have been able to avoid the worst of the turmoil.

If like J. P. Morgan, America's ultimate financier, or George Bernard Shaw, you happen to look exactly like yourself, you'll probably get exactly what you deserve from other people. Shaw's face could hardly have suited his personality better if he had designed it himself, and I haven't a doubt that in part he did. He could have been cast in any play that required a quizzical, provocative, brilliant playwright. And J.P. could have starred in any role calling for a prosperous, dignified tycoon striking terror in the heart of any opponent. He had piercing eyes "like the lights of an oncoming express train . . . a bulbous, flaming nose," and sat "like a huge baleful dragon, not posing but confronting the camera." He ran American finance as if he owned the country, which in a way he did. He couldn't believe it when a mere president of the United States, Theodore Roosevelt, planned to break up one of his trusts. He left immediately for Washington, chastised the young man severely for making a move without warning him, and treated the president as "a big rival operator." He returned to New York expressing the opinion that T.R. was a lunatic, worse than a socialist.

Most of us, however, are not so clearly revealed by our outward appearance and need to be alert, patient, and helpful with those who have trouble finding us beneath the skin.

But back to my silly patient who is so conceited she thinks everybody's going to be focusing on her flaws and, therefore, nobody will ever love her. Now, enter some poor unsuspecting man who has no idea the trouble he's about to see. He just likes the lift of her chin or her crooked smile (with the mixed-up teeth) or who knows what. He invites her for a cup of coffee. Of course, she's far too worried about how she's coming across to see him as anything more than a judge of her loveability. But even though she's been totally self-centered, he's still attracted and asks her for a date. (If he hadn't, she'd have known it was her looks that turned him off.)

Now we come to the date, which isn't an ordinary, garden-variety date, a chance to see whether two people hit it off as well as they guessed they might. Not to my patient. It's the final, ultimate, irrevocable verdict on her ability to attract a man. Heaven forbid, he should have a moment's doubt. She doesn't think she's beautiful, but God help him, if he doesn't, or fails to call exactly as often as she needs him to. Meanwhile, sauce for the goose (and what a little goose) is clearly not sauce for the gander, for there she sits in my office listing his every negative feature. (She had after all been thinking of a prince, and he's kind of scrawny and red-haired, and maybe he's never going to be rich, and he made mistakes in grammar.)

Yet she likes the guy and might even end up loving him. But when I suggest mildly that it might be fair to let him have a few negative feelings about her too, that's a different story altogether. However, if she can stop assuming she's mortally wounded every time he is even faintly unaccepting or disinterested, the relationship can run along to its rightful outcome, which could be anything—they separate by mutual consent, she rejects him, he rejects her, they get married—who knows. It will turn out however it ought to turn out, if I can persuade her that we ought to be able to take as bad as we hand out, which in our thoughts, at least, is often pretty bad. Suppose your boss were free to be as hard on you as you are on him in your thoughts. I have a friend of whom her friends say, "If you didn't love her, you wouldn't be able to stand her," which is a verdict we all ought to be willing to accept sometimes.

Now for a few home truths about rejection. First, everybody's doing it and everybody's getting it. There's no possible escape. There is nobody you don't reject—in part. Your dearest love has some physical attributes or personality quirks you don't enjoy or admire—or that even drive you up the wall. You can be 99 percent certain with a new acquaintance that you are going to be rejected sometime, for something, for as you look at strangers, your own computer is ticking away like a daisy petal counter: like—don't like—like—like—don't like—like, or some such verdict at every word they say, every bit of knowledge you accumulate about them, every detail of their appearance. If we understand this, then we learn to accept rejection when we must, not just as evidence of our failure or inferiority, but as a normal part of relationships. They are always a gamble. The people who understand this and are brave enough to take their losses, finally find the people among whom they really belong. But many people are lonely failures all their lives because they couldn't stand being rejected a few or maybe a lot of times on the road to finding the ideal job or the ideal mate.

And people who are ashamed of their bodies or their faces are terribly vulnerable. They interpret the normal wear and tear of building relationships as evidence that the quest is hopeless, which is too bad since, if they have serious flaws, they may in reality be rejected more often than other people and therefore may need an extra dose of common sense, stamina, and self-regard.

A very pretty girl from Texas had a slight limp and a slightly disabled hand. She could not endure traveling on a bus because she felt everybody was staring and feeling sorry for her because she was crippled. (Some of this could have been true, I suppose. The eye tends to follow anything that's unusual.) Gradually, she began to feel more comfortable with herself and to socialize. I was pleased, but thought I'd check. So I asked her if people still stared at her on the bus. She replied, "Yes, they do sometimes," and her voice rose indignantly, "especially the men." I laughed heartlessly and told her I had no remedy for that affliction, that I thought she was always going to be noticed by girl-watchers.

I suppose more people get rejected for not liking themselves than for any other flaw. It makes one very wary if an owner won't stand behind the product but expects us to tell him whether its any good, yet many people with defects expect other people to accept the flaws better than they themselves do. They say, in effect, "If you'll just like me then I'll be broad-minded and like me too." I suspect that's what the story of the frog prince is all about. We long for someone to accept us and enable us to see ourselves transformed into the wonderful person we've always wanted to be. And love often does that. But generally if we see ourselves as frogs, other people do too.

People who are embarrassed, apologetic, or bitter about their disabilities usually disturb us more by their discomfort than by their defects. We are always a little frightened by other people's troubles, fearing what could happen to us too. If they are ashamed, crushed, or obsequious they frighten us even more. When they can cope and respect and enjoy being themselves, in spite of the flaws, this reassures us not only about them but about us, and their defects fade into the background of our relationship.

The game of life may be won by those who have been dealt magnificent hands but, as this book demonstrates, it's usually won by the best players, no matter how the cards have fallen. And playing to win, even with a poor hand, can make a rewarding and exhilarating life. (And a good player always knows how to keep his losses to an absolute minimum.)

You are, after all, in all time and space, the only sample of you. That in itself seems to me tremendously exciting: to seek out the possibilities for this unique phenomenon. And only you will be in a position to judge how well you have succeeded and to hand out the prizes. Other people may admire an achievement that in fact was easy for you, while nobody but you may ever know how hard an apparently easy accomplishment was.

I know a young man who has no idea how magnificently he has succeeded because he has always measured himself by other people's standards. He is a very bright man making excellent headway in a challenging profession, and since he's the first in his family to go beyond the fourth grade, he's had to do it on his own. Furthermore, he comes from a home that was terrifyingly dangerous, and every inch of his progress, from the terror of being a first grader who couldn't understand English to the terror of his first address at a technical conference, has been a battle against the frightened child he once was. Yet instead of feeling intense pride and self-confidence, awarding himself medals for extreme bravery under fire, he often feels ashamed and inferior. You see, he measures himself not against other men with the same obstacles, but against his friends who were the pampered darlings of very literate and ambitious parents and who were spoon-fed all the education and social graces which he has had to acquire for himself. (But how facilely they talk. How exactly they know what to do on social occasions. He never notices *their* weaknesses, their hothouse quality.) Yet a small change of perspective could transform his nerve-wracking struggle into the adventure of a happy warrior, for when the game is played for itself, winning against odds can be great fun.

Like this young man, many a famous man continues to feel bitter and degraded over physical imperfections that have become inconsequential or actually magnify his success. For if you are very good or very bad, your defects make you look even better or worse. Without his crutch, Tiny Tim could probably never have had such a goody-goody reputation. He'd have been seen as just one more mischievous little Cratchit. And the pegleg did wonders for Long John Silver, evil-image–wise.

What did Byron's lame leg really cost him? Perhaps soccer stardom and the acceptance of one woman out of a thousand. Yet, partly at least, because of it, Byron sentenced himself to exile for life from his own affection and self-regard. But as I told you, the worst part of people with physical imperfections is often their heads. If that is screwed on right, nature can try its damnedest and still get circumvented. What Arthur Macmurrough Kavanaugh did to his Fate was enough to give it a permanent inferiority complex. Without any limbs, he seems to have outdistanced most of his physically normal contemporaries on almost every test by which we evaluate the achievement, worth, and happiness of a life.

Then think of Alexander Pope. He became a great poet and, despite his obnoxiousness, had some quality that gave him a group of true friends and at least one woman who truly loved him. But imagine the difference to this man's life if he had not been warped in spirit as well as in body; if he had, like Kavanaugh, been able to accept people's initial reaction without bitterness, secure in the knowledge that it's the long run, not the first impression, that counts.

While one has to cope, no one should ever have to apologize for what nature or accident has made him, or for that matter, what he has done to himself, so long as it does not impinge upon other people. If he's fat, that's his business. Yet many people who are fat feel guilty and, thereby, encourage bullying. They are just beginning to see they've made themselves a downtrodden minority by their acceptance of discrimination and their unwillingness to fight back. A credo of "Myself—may I ever be flawless; but Myself—flawless or not" isn't a bad idea. Loyalty to oneself through thick and thin is not only very helpful to the owner of flaws but to those who deal with him. It tends to make both sides forget the disability except for its practical limitations. Everybody focused on Byron's foot, everybody forgot Sir Walter Scott's; that's the difference between a personal traitor and a personal loyalist.

There is only one person whose rejection can ruin your life—yourself. Other people can cause grief and disappointment, or can make us lonely, but if they do not turn us against ourselves, we'll survive very well. And it's been my observation that people who accept and enjoy themselves are terribly attractive to other people, no matter how they look.

If You Would Like
to Know More

For readers who may be interested in a particular flaw or who wish to dip further into the history of medical research, a small picture of the research and its sources is provided. (This, of course, only covers a small fraction of the material actually researched and used.)

Many items were dug out, one by one, from ancient and modern reports of conferences where medical historians fought furiously in scholarly gobbletygook over George Washington's teeth or the historical significance of Napoleon's hemorrhoids. (And what does the serial number on the Duke of Wellington's dentures mean?) Then came the journals such as the *Annals of Medical History* and more battles. And on to the old books, like the lucky find of E. M. Gould's *Biographic Clinics* wherein this turn-of-the-century eye specialist gives excellent accounts of the ailments of Darwin, Carlyle, and that whole crowd of great thinkers, and concludes that *all* of their ailments came from astigmatism! The medical gossip of the French court is served in even older books by A. Cabanes: *Curious Bypaths of History* and *The Secret Cabinet of History Peeped Into by a Doctor.*

Then came the books that cover a range of history, flaws, and social gossip like *X-Raying the Pharaohs* by J. E. Harris and K. R. Weeks; *The World That Was India* by A. L. Bashan; *Hero Dust* and *Idols and Invalids* by J. Kemble; *Great Abnormals* by T. B. Hyslop; *Genius and Disaster* by J. Marks; *An American Biographic Clinic: The Lame, the Halt, and the Celebrated* by S. Epstein; *A Doctor Looks at Life and History* by D. S. Mickle; and *The Decline and Fall of Practically Everybody* by W. Cuppy. The gossip of the 18th and 19th centuries provided an assortment of flaws in: *The Great Corinthian* by D. Leslie on the Georges III and IV, their wives, relatives, friends and enemies: *The Creevey Papers*, edited by J. Gore; and Harriette Wilson's *Memoirs*, the same scene through the eyes of a fashionable courtesan.

Then, in search of particular flaws, we found (among many others):

On HAIR, *Hair, Sex, and Symbolism* by W. Cooper gives a wealth of oddities plus anthropological and psychoanalytic interpretations; *Once Over Lightly: The Story of a Man and His Hair* by C. De Zemler is the loving tribute of a barber to the history of his profession.

On EYES, there was *A History of Spectacles* by J. E. Lebensohn, and two lovely books: *A Gross of Green Spectacles* by C. S. Flick and P. Trevor-Roper's *The World Through Blunted Vision* (including the vision of artists).

On TEETH, by a dentist, S. Garfield, who had fun writing it, *Teeth, Teeth, Teeth;* M. K. Bremner's *The Story of Dentistry* (hard to come by but good); V. Guercino's *History of Dentistry;* and B. W. Weinberg's two-volume *An Introduction to the History of Dentistry.* And finally we came to the *Memoirs* of John Greenwood, Washington's favorite dentist, and *Dentistry and Its Victims* by, of all people, Paul Revere.

On EARS, NOSES, and FACES, *Our Noses* by W. Martin; "Ear, Nose and Face Prostheses" in *Otolaryngology* by Hagestown; and *The Hearing Aid and Its Development* by K. W. Berger. The fun with physiognomy—the Victorian was found in J. Simms' *Physiognomy Illustrated*, and the ancient Chinese in W. A. Lessa's *Chinese Body Divination*.

On HANDS and FEET, about sports figures with impairments, there is *Sports Heroes Who Wouldn't Quit* by H. Butler and *Glorious Triumphs* by V. Pizer; "Amputations and Prostheses Through the Centuries" by B. J. Ficarra in *Essays on Historical Medicine* is also good. But the real find was Arthur Macmurrough Kavanaugh, first encountered in M. McCarthy's *Handicaps: Six Studies*.

On SKIN, any book of unretouched pictures of famous people, especially those by Y. Karsh. The one mentioned here is *Portraits of Greatness; The Pageant of Elizabethan England* by E. Burton (a delightful book). Also try *Elizabeth the First, Queen of England* by N. Williams.

On SIZE, *It's a Small World* by W. Bodin, on the smallest people; *Giants and Dwarfs* by E. J. Wood; *Dr Darwin* by H. Pearson; *Frederick the Great* by N. Mitford (for the story of the regiment of giants); and *Little Men in Sports* by L. Fox.

On MEDICAL AILMENTS, there were *The Health of the Presidents* by R. Marx; *Thirteen Famous Patients* by N. D. Fabricant; *Medical Biographies; the Ailments of Thirty-Three Famous Persons* by P. M. Dale; *The Glands of Destiny* by I. V. Cobbs; Roche Products Limited's *Famous People and Their Illnesses*, and a little volume by Abeshous, *Troubled Waters*, on famous bladders and their problems.

Having finished with flaws, we go on to people, love and romance: with *Napoleon the Immortal* by J. Kemble; *Louis XIV in Love and War* by S. Huddleston; *Twelve Royal Ladies* by S. Dark; and *Living Biographies of Famous Rulers* and *Biographies of Famous Women*, both by H. and D. Thomas. The wives of the first presidents are the *First First Ladies* by M. O. Whitton, and M. W. Goodwin writes of one of them in *Dolly Madison*.

The story of Elizabeth and Robert Browning is well told in

The Immortal Lovers by F. Winwar. George Eliot's story is in A. Ewart's *The World's Great Love Affairs*, *The School of Femininity* by M. Lawrence, and *George Eliot the Woman* by M. Crompton. *Wingless Victory* by F. Winwar is the tale of D'Annunzio and Duse. *Sir Richard Burton's Wife* by J. Burton is a warm and funny telling of their romance. There is no completely satisfactory story of Irving and Ellin Berlin, because he wishes no biography except by his wife and only after his death.

Of the great Don Juans, Rasputin is well described in *Nicholas and Alexandra* by R. Massie, and there are several early versions including that by the assassin, and one by the priest who punched him. I like Byron in *The Fatal Gift of Beauty*, the last years of Byron and Shelley in Italy by A. B. C. Whipple. The *Casanova* of J. R. Childs is good and there are Casanova's own *Memoirs of Jacques Casanova*, edited by E. Boyd.

Index

252

Index

Bismarck, 19
Bogart, Humphrey, 224-25, 232
Boleyn, Anne, 45, 76-77
Bolivar, Simon, 133
Bonaparte, Napoleon. *See* Napoleon
Booth, Evangeline, 58
Booth, Junius, 224
Borden, Lizzie, 61
Bourbon, Duc de, 34-35
Boyer, Charles, 232
Brahmins, 2-3
Brahms, Johannes, 105
Braque, 32
Brawne, Fanny, 156, 196-97
Bray, Charles, 176
Brinkley, David, 98
British Medical Journal, 153
Brougham, Lord, 94
Brown, Mordecai (Three Finger), 80
Browning, Elizabeth Barrett, 172-75
Browning, Robert, 173-75
Brunswick, Duchess of, 166
Brynner, Yul, 10
Buchanan, James, 28, 62
Buddha, Gautama, 44, 47
Bunyan, John, 23
Burr, Aaron, 133, 179
Burton, Isabel, 183-87
Burton, Sir Richard Francis, 183-87
Byron, Lord, 82, 140, 200, 210-18, 220, 244, 245

Caesar, Julius, 4, 104, 137, 149
Caligula, 106
Calvus, Licenius, 128
Camus, Albert, 61, 118
Canute, King, 104
Caracus, 128
Carlisle, William, 62
Carlyle, Thomas, 153
Carnegie, Andrew, 132
Casanova, 69, 220, 223, 224
Cascellius, 40
Castro, Fidel, 16
Catherine the Great, 34
Chamberlain, Wilt, 132
Chancellor, John, 98
Charlemagne, 128, 148
Charles I, 129, 131
Charles II, 5, 151-52, 198

Charles V (of Spain), 26, 130, 151
Chatos, King, 6
Chaucer, 108, 132
Child, Julia, 125
Chilperic, King, 129
Chopin, Frederic, 16, 133
Churchill, Winston, 61, 106-107
Cicero, 128
Cinesios, 74-75
Claremont, Claire, 214
Cleopatra, 17, 171
Clotilda, Queen, 3
Codman, Dr., 41
Colgate, James Booman, 11-12
Colgate, Samuel, 12
Columbus, Christopher, 104
Constable, James, 12
Constable (John), 33
Constantine, Emperor, 104
Cooke-Taylor, Dr., 101
Copernicus, 107
Corder, William, 114
Correggio, 105
Cortez, 104
Cosmus, Saint, 42
Coustau, Benjamin, 232
Couvisant, Dr., 41
Coventry, Lady, 115
Craig, Gordon, 19
Croes, Dr., 160
Croesus, 128
Cromwell, Oliver, 108-109, 119, 152
Cronkite, Walter, 98
Cuvilles, Jean Francois de, 131-32
Cuvilles, Jean Francois de, Jr., 132

D'Annunzio, Gabriele, 188, 189-91
Darwin, Charles, 137-40, 153-54
Darwin, Dr. Erasmus, 137
Daumier, 31
Davies, Sir Humphrey, 83
Davis, Sammy, Jr., 34
Dayan, General Moishe, 34
de Ayald, Perico, 130
de Caumont, Antoine Nompar, 218-20
Degas (Edgar), 32
de Gevara, Cardinal Inquisitor Nino, 23
Delmonico, 11